YES, ONLY TO THE RIGHT PERSON

Copyright © 2016. All rights reserved.

No part of this publication may be reproduced, stored in a retrieval system or transmitted in any way by any means, electronic, mechanical, photocopy, recording or otherwise, without the prior permission of the author except as provided by USA copyright law.

All characters appearing in this work are fictitious. Any resemblance to real persons, living or dead, is purely coincidental.

The opinions expressed by the author are not necessarily those of Revival Waves of Glory Books & Publishing.

Published by Revival Waves of Glory Books & Publishing

PO Box 596 | Litchfield, Illinois 62056 USA

www.revivalwavesofgloryministries.com

Revival Waves of Glory Books & Publishing is committed to excellence in the publishing industry.

Book design Copyright © 2016 by Revival Waves of Glory Books & Publishing. All rights reserved.

Published in the United States of America

Paperback: 978-1684111770

YES, ONLY TO THE RIGHT PERSON

A Guide to Choosing the Right Partner

O.D. Chimex

Contents

Foreword 8

Part One: Positive Qualities

Introduction 12

Quality 1: Makes You Better; Achieving Better Goals 1

Quality 2: Personality Makes the Person Love the More 6

Quality 3: Romance Not Too Quick to Start 11

Quality 4: Time Makes It Stronger 16

Quality 5: Warns You of Danger 21

Quality 6: Being Generous 26

Quality 7: Being Altruistic 31

Quality 8: Does Not Keep A Count of Wrongs 36

Quality 9: Letting Your Opinion Count 41

Quality 10: Doesn't Pay Attention to Your Flaws 46

Quality 11: Settles Disagreement in a Short Time 51

Quality 12: Being Submissive 56

Quality 13: Being Humorous 61

Part Two: Negative Signs (Danger signs)

Introduction 67

Sign 1: Makes You Do What is Bad 69

Sign 2: Makes Material Request From You Always 74

Sign 3: Takes Offense at Every Little Thing 79

Sign 4: Slow About Initiating Conversation 83

Sign 5: Argument Becomes the Order of the Day 88

Sign 6: Derogatory Words Without Feeling Remorse 93

Sign 7: Intense Jealousy 98

Sign 8: Constant Criticism of Your Efforts 103

Sign 9: Being Aggressive 108

Sign 10: Being Restrictive 113

Sign 11: Physical Appearance is the Reason for Loving 118

Sign 12: Belittles You 123

Sign 13: Sweet Words Start Immediately 128

Sign 14: Does Not Yield 132

Sign 15: Being Manipulative 137

Sign 16: Being Possessive 142

Sign 17: Being Quarrelsome 147

Part Three: Knowing This Person Better

Introduction 153

Tool 1: How This Person Treats Others 155

Tool 2: How This Person Handles Authority 160

Tool 3: The Person's Goals 165

Tool 4: The Person's Friends 170

Tool 5: What This Person Always Talks About 175

Tool 6: The Person's Scale of Preference 180

Tool 7: The Person's Hobby 185

Tool 8: The Person's Job 190

Tool 9: How the Person Handles Resources 195

Tool 10: The Person's Addiction 200
Tool 11: The Person's Grooming................................. 205

Part Four: Making Yourself That Right Person
Introduction 212
Step 1: Your Mindset 213
Step 2: Your Speech... 219
Step 3: Your Character 225

Foreword

"A loving relationship is one which the loved one is free to be himself – to laugh with me, but never at me; to cry with me, but never because of me; to love life, to love himself, to love being loved. Such a relationship is based upon real love with the right person and there is freedom, and it will never die." - Leo F. Buscaglia.

You go on being in the wrong relationship; it seems to you that all men are the same, that all women are the same. You are blurred as to knowing the proper somebody. After that disastrous end of your last relationship you are sceptical about starting a relationship. What if you just want to start a relationship, maybe this is your first, you really don't want to make mistakes and get hurt like others. Now you have this particular person who wants to make you his partner and you want to give it a try, but you are confused as to how to get to know if this person will be the right person. You are bent on not making a wrong decision. Not to worry, that sure help you need is just right in your face, only for you to take hold of it.

Issues related to dating, relationship and marriage are taken so seriously by rational people, because they know that they could be marred or made by this. Intrinsically we all yearn to spend the rest of our life with the right person, which will undoubtedly bring happiness into our life. A resolve we have made to search out for the right person. Sadly, we are somehow handicapped when searching out for this right person due to the overbearing influence of our emotions, which sometimes deceive us. These emotions go a long way to make us overlook danger signs in a person, and in the end, we get hurt. Although some people are lucky enough to fortuitously get to be with the right person. Many also basked in the euphoria, thought they were with the right person, only to get disappointed at last. That everywhere you look, you see people in relationship and they seem to be with the right persons, does not mean they are with the right person. The truth remains that some of them are with the wrong persons unknowingly, and they may likely meet an impasse at last. The skyrocketing rate of breakups and divorces will testify to this, that really, people are often, hasten climbers and they actually sudden fall.

It might be that you have tried many times your possible best to search for the right person, but you often fail to find the right person because you have no yardstick to assess this person. It might be that at the start, the person seemed to be the right person, but as the relationship went on, reality set in that you were with the wrong person. Is it your fault then? Should you be blamed for being with the wrong person? Can you actually be with the right person? Can you find real love? The responses to these questions remain absolute YES. It is your fault; you have refused to acquaint yourself with the qualities that make one a right person. It is your fault for being with the wrong person because you have failed to avail yourself of the danger signs of the wrong person. It is possible to find the right person, and possible to stay in the right relationship, finding true love. But then, it will only be very possible when you have the basic hints at your fingertips that you can easily find out if the person is the right one. If you are already in a relationship, this is the time to begin this assessment. Instead of continuing blindly in love heading for a disastrous breakup in the near future, why not assess this person thoroughly, if he is the right person. The best option for you is to break up now if you get to find out this person is the wrong person. Instead of naively investing your emotions in the wrong person, why not rightly invest your time in searching for the right one? Instead of heading for a doomed marriage, why not weigh your relationship and see if you really are with the right person. The already married ones were not left out entirely, they can as well weigh their marriage, assess their partners, and see the areas it is found wanting, and then, try as much as possible to bridge that lacuna before it heads for doom.

This four-part book is a sure help to solve that problem of assessing this person if he will be the right person for you. It gives in details, the qualities of the right person with which one can weigh a potential or already partner. It goes on to discuss the danger signs that the wrong person will always exhibit; detailing the other tools with which to see the real person and not what he makes you believe. And finally, the last part which has to do with working on yourself, to as well make a right person for a relationship. This book will take you by the hand and guide you in making an honest appraisal of this person to see if he is qualified as the right partner for you. Remember relationship is like that beautiful clothe you see at the shopping mall; no matter how pretty it is and how you have fallen in love with it, it must be the right one, I mean, your size, before you can purchase it and enjoy it. If it is not your size, no matter how you try to force it on yourself, you will always be uncomfortable. "No one can hurt me without my permission." Just like Mahatma Gandhi has said it; you can give someone that permission unknowingly to hurt you. Rise up above the sky now and do not give someone that permission to hurt you, by availing yourself of this checklist. I bet you, after reading this book; you can only be in a relationship with the wrong person, if you choose to.

NB: For the sake of simplicity and fluency, the pronoun **HE** is used often to refer to both male and female; and it used also in the illustrations and experiences. This book is not gender biased.

Part One
Positive Qualities

Introduction

"Flatter me, and I may not believe you. Criticize me, and I may not like you. Ignore me, and I may not forgive you. Encourage me, and I will not forget you. Love me, and I may be forced to love you." - William Arthur Ward.

The journey to a perfect relationship starts a day, but does not end in a day. It should be a sweet journey that continues till both parties reach a destination, that is marriage. What makes this journey a sweet and true one is when some positive qualities are present in a partner to embellish the journey. These positive qualities, one should take notice of so as to know if a person is the right partner for the journey. This section treats, particularly those positive qualities one sees in a partner that will make the journey not only sweet, but with purpose making it a perfect one that will be enjoyed till that destination is reached. These signs, when most of them are seen in a person, shows that the person is likely the right person and that the relationship is the right one. Though one might not expect to see them all in a partner, but if a partner has most of them, that person might likely make the best partner for the journey and that the relationship is likely going to take the two to that destination.

Quality 1

Makes You Better; Achieving Better Goals

Love is when you meet someone who tells you something new about yourself." - **Andre Breton.**

We cannot run away from this important fact that conduciveness breeds productivity. The more you find yourself in an enabling environment, the more chances that you will do better. And this conduciveness will be climaxed when you have human resources to support it. It happens also in a relationship when you are in the right one with the right person. This is the reason kids from a better home do better at school than kids from a bad home; the same with relationships. If one is in a good relationship there is every possibility that such a person will do better, improving positively. This sign of knowing if you are in the right relationship with the right person makes is glaring that the more you get to know the other person and the relationship grows, the more you see yourself improving and doing what you wouldn't have ordinarily done on your own. You feel that support and love to achieve better plans because the atmosphere is very conducive for positivity, and your heart and brain feel safe. This comes naturally, you don't need to fight for it since you are happy that you

YES, ONLY TO THE RIGHT PERSON

entrusted your heart to the right person. You will see that this partner will always augment you being an addition to you mentally and psychologically. That is the power of a team work. When you have a perfect colleague working alongside you at work, you are likely going to achieve better than when you are just working alone. Humans are meant to complement each other, and this works perfectly when two good people are working together to achieve a particular goal. Both will be seeing themselves improving and the task as well, day in day out.

Citing this phrase becomes appropriate: "that iron sharpens iron." Yes, this is also very applicable in a good relationship. One who is the right person will always sharpen you making you a better person. You see yourself achieving what ordinarily you wouldn't have achieved on your own. You see yourself positively making visible improvements in all ramifications. It is because you now have a true helper who is your perfect complement. This person is in essence proving to you that he is that better half of you. What else do you want in a relationship than a person that will make you be that best of you. This complementarity comes in many ways. Some may come in the form of advice improving your plans and characters, encouraging words, making you achieve things that looked impossible if you were alone, and support, when you feel you cannot do it anymore. And most will even come as a result of having the conduciveness that your body and mind need, to think and plan better. This right person keeps making you do more and more and achieve more beyond your wildest dream. He becomes your foundation making you fly without wings. And when you think you have every reason to quit, he says 'no you can do it.'

Most people keep saying that behind any successful man there is a woman and behind any successful woman also there is a man. This shows that every successful person has a supporter. And what more do you need from your partner than to support your good plans? This right person will always make you see that potential that you need to tap into. He does it because he loves you and has concern for your wellbeing.

His priority is to see you succeed and not see you fail. And when you fail, you have someone to take hold of your hand and make you continue. How heartwarming it is when you are running on the track and such voice of your partner is thundering from the crowd cheering you to keep running. This same person who has proved to be a real partner will as well not desert you when every other person has deserted you.

A relationship with the right person should not always distract you with lots to worry making you sick, rather it should always disturb you with lots of things you should do so as to achieve your dreams and aspiration. To your left, you have someone telling you: "Yes, you can achieve it. And to your right, that same voice is telling you to soar like an eagle in the sky: "Yes, you have all it takes to do it." And with this support, you think you won't be better achieving better goals? More of the reason some couples these days like to go into the labour room together, because the sight of the other person makes the one in labour to have confidence to surmount any challenge. This reminds me of this popular proverb that my dad always cites: "A child sent by his dad even to go steal, always breaks the door with just a kick with the leg." Having a right person with you, makes you do the right thing with confidence. This goes a long way to make you see reason some kids are very confident outside the home, maybe at school or at any other places, because they are very sure that they have enough backup as parents to sort their mess out.

That right person is very supportive even when you think you have failed, yet you see this person telling you that you did right, correcting you lovingly when necessary. When others are jeering you, that person is there cheering you and it makes you to do more despite challenges. In your heart too, you really don't want to put this special person down, you are very afraid to let him down, so you ought to do your best to make this person proud, and this boils down to achieving great things. Imagine when you want to venture into something and you remember

YES, ONLY TO THE RIGHT PERSON

how happy you will make this special person when you finally succeed. You think how this very thing will bring enormous benefit to this wonderful person; then your best is needed. That is what right relationship makes you do, because the other person matter a lot in your life. Your aim will be to make this relationship work because you see reasons to do so. Those efforts go a long way to better you, the relationship and your partner; in the end, you will only be rewarded with happiness. This is like a circular flow diagram in a relationship.

To buttress this fact, let us take for example, a child that really loves his parents so much that he wants them always happy all the time. This child for the fact that he puts his parents' happiness ahead of him will make him to do excellently well in school, because he wants dad and mom to give him that wonderful hug and peck saying, they are very proud of him. This child is unknowingly setting a policy of winning in his heart, and that becomes the order of the day in his life. The more the child tries to please mom and dad, the more efforts he puts and the more he achieves a lot. But a child that hates his parents will always think: "To hell with whatever you feel about me, I don't really care." And that child puts no effort to do things that will make his parents happy. And when this becomes a way of life for the child, a declining movement becomes the other of the day in his life as well. Same takes place when with the right person in a right relationship. This person makes the environment to be conducive for you, shows you every good reason that you are important. In return you are motivated and you pay back by not letting this person down.

For the fact that you have the right person standing beside you will give you the needed impetus to achieve great things. And for the fact that you value this person so much will also make you to put effort to make him so proud of you. And this is the formula in a right relationship with the right person. The person directly and indirectly influences you to achieve great height without knowing. But the wrong person seem to be the other way round, putting you down, causing disaster in the environment thereby making you to dissipate your energy in sorting out the mess. You on the other hand, will not be willing to put effort to make this person happy. Believe it or not, you are bound to become a far better person with the right person knowingly or unknowingly.

Quality 2

Personality Makes the Person Love the More

"They say love is blind, I agree; which is why I am blind to see how you look outside." - **O.D. Chimex.**

Seeing only the physical appearance of a person is always synonymous with either people that are wrong, or with people that are either kids by age or in brain. Before going further I will like to narrate this childhood experience. Clara was a beautiful young girl I admired during my school days at the elementary level. Each time I set my eyes on this girl, I felt a force pulling me toward her like a magnetic force. Then I was so young like twelve years old. What really attracted me to Clara I could not just say then, the only thing I could remember is that my heart yearned for Clara's beautiful appearance those school days. But how naïve I was to base such fake love on just physical appearance. To say that I loved Clara then was the biggest lie I could tell myself now. All I had for her was just a mere infatuation, because my so called love had no basis, not even a single block as the foundation. This happened in the first term, and when we went on holiday, on resumption of the second term, the whole feelings died in me. The truth is that I was more obsessed with her very imposing physical appearance like those models I watched in a television then, and when I stopped seeing her for long, the obsession fainted. If a person is for real, his reason for loving you should be based on your wonderful personality.

Today many find themselves in the same obsession on physical appearance in the name of love; this is not the same with the right person. Though the first attraction might be physical attributes, but then when the love is real, you will find out that what makes this person yearn to continue in the relationship is not again your physical appearance. He has seen wonderful qualities that relationship needs, and this makes him to continue loving you. These unseen qualities vividly felt by the person form the basis for wanting to continue in the relationship. This is why you may see someone casual with a person, and before you know it, he becomes too serious and wants to take the relationship to a higher level. It is not just the workings of the emotions, but it is about seeing things unseen. When a person behaves in a manner or say things that show that your inner personality is the reason for wanting to be serious, then you have every reason to believe that this person is for real. A real relationship is based on those qualities unseen, and only the right person takes this into consideration.

Most times, wrong people are interested in just the physical attributes of a person, and this they tend to always voice out. But there are more to the physical appearance that the right person will come to notice, and will continue to be drawn closer due to those sterling qualities. Imagine when this person is alone, and fantasizing you, what first comes to his mind is nothing but how beautiful you are physically. Your beautiful or handsome face? Your voluptuous figure or muscular body? Your smiles? These are the only things that such wrong person always notices. How foolish it is to think that such a person will make a better partner. What if, someone continues to remind you that what draws you closer to him and make him dread losing you are those invisible sterling qualities of yours. Will you not be convinced that this

YES, ONLY TO THE RIGHT PERSON

person really have a foundation for professing love? These qualities are what differentiate a person from others; making someone to stand out. Imagine if such person could liken your qualities to that of his loving mother or father, how dear you will continue to be in his heart. What if you get to know that he likens you to his wonderful sibling? These are people that make great difference in someone's life and are so cherished and loved, love for them will never fade away. If you have a person who could insinuate or tell you he sees you as those wonderful family members of his, due to your inner qualities that are like those, how assuring it will be that you will as well be special just like those people. This kind of person is what a real partner should be like, loving people for what they are inside, drawing inference to his parents or sibling.

The more he gets to know you, the more he sees those wonderful qualities you have that will make him to fall head over in love. This shows that you are with someone that is for real. Such a person will continue to hold you in high esteem just like those special people in his life. Your convenience will be very paramount to such person, the same way those family members' will. No doubt that such a person will continue to voice out how wonderful your qualities have attracted him to you. A person like this makes you always feel at home, even when you think that a disagreement is so serious to dent the relationship, you will be surprise knowing that you both can still work it out. If a particular land is found to have deposit of some precious stones, the owner will always find it hard to let go of such land. When a person sees you as that land with vast deposit of hidden treasures, how hard to let you go. This does not mean that the physical attributes will totally be forgotten, but it shows that what matters is the inner person and that is the foundation of a good relationship.

He will come to the conclusion that you are more beautiful inwardly than outwardly and this is the evidence that the love is solidly built. Only a right person will build a love based on inner qualities of a person. This kind of love built on the inner person lasts longer than the one built on the outer person. It is very obvious that physical appearance will not continue to be the same day after day, but the inner person gets more beautiful by the day. And for this fact, real love is bound to be based on that inner person and not that outer person. This is the reason you have to really examine why someone professes love for you. And if 90% of his reasons are based on your personality, then you are with someone that will make a right person. Although age might again come against this judgment, like the story told at the beginning of this topic, when one is very young and naïve, the person tends to base his judgment on the physical qualities. But the truth still remains that if one is really honest to himself, he should give more attention to the inner person and not the outer person when going into a relationship.

Humans though sometimes look alike outwardly, but they tend to show that they are more beautiful than others inwardly. And if this person weighs this, loving you by your inner qualities, the person is showing that right attitude that a good relationship needs. You don't need to search too long to get this answer, this person's utterances will continue to show what attracts him to you. What makes him want to love you the more and want to build on the relationship, should be your personality. This will either show you that the person might be an actor, or for real. With someone who loves you due to your personality, as situations arise in relationship, you will find him showing that he is such a right person with right intentions for you. This is not just a mere fantasy love like the one portrayed in the movies and in the super love stories books. He sees you as the most beautiful person in the world; this is how it supposed to be because judgment is based on your personality. And if you are to be placed side by side with most superb looking models, he won't waste time to pick you as his choice, because your personality will always stand out from those others.

This is why sometimes, people will see a couple and will be astonished as to why one has chosen to be in a relationship with the other. It is simple, the person is more beautiful inside than outside, and

YES, ONLY TO THE RIGHT PERSON

you watching didn't see that. The truth remains that real love is not based on physical attributes but the inner attributes which will likely distinguish a person from another. Only a person with right intentions will come to understand this fact, and that he will continue to express this in actions and in words. The right person loves the inner you more than he loves the outer you.

Quality 3

Romance Not Too Quick to Start

"I think it's love when your heart matters and not your ass; your feelings matter and not your body; and it matters to first love you and not to first lay you. And this love is built in the heart and not in the bed." -O.D. Chimex.

Romance, a very important aspect of a relationship, but some people always abuse it to the detriment of a relationship as well. When we say romance, we mean sexual activities that come when two people are professing love for each other in a relationship. In the world of moral decay like ours, romance has become the only key that people think will give them access into that house called relationship. But then, that is a misnomer. Romance is not meant to be the key that will give you access into the house; it should be the padlock to lock the house with when you both are secure inside, probably when serious commitment has been made. In fact, this has become a very important yardstick for measuring when one is with the right person or with the wrong person. In the right relationship with the right person, romance takes time to start and not too quick. Ponder over these questions: "Does this one always seek out every opportunity to feast on you, just like a swarm of locust? Is your body the first point of call whenever you are close to each other? If this be the case, then this is just a bad omen.

YES, ONLY TO THE RIGHT PERSON

For with the right person, it shouldn't be so quick. Do not be deceived thinking it is just the body chemistry showing that you both are compatible. No it is not; this is just a very simple and glaring way to tell you that, look this person is just after your body to satisfy himself; and that when obstacles come, the person will just back off. Think of what will happen when you keep telling the person to leave off your body; you are in essence telling the person to leave you. He will not even blink an eye to leave you when he becomes sure that your body is not available at the moment.

Although you are handicapped by feelings, but then the right person is not just interested in your body first, that is not the first thing in the person's scale of preference. He comes to love you and not to lay you. Take a look at this illustration to make this fact clearer. You have just seen a very beautiful car in a showroom, and you have the wherewithal to make this car your own; yes your credit card and your checkable deposit are large enough to accommodate the purchase at this moment you saw the car. Again, you need this car badly; you have been longing to drive a car for long. Boisterously you walked into the showroom and the price tag is placed on the body. Fortunately you even have enough cash in your pocket to pay for it, and there you go. Off to the account department, dropping the money on the desk and racing towards the partition, taking the car key hung and off you drove away. The car is yours now; after all you have paid for it. If the cops didn't go after you at that moment, then probably they are on strike. You really have to follow the legitimate procedures if you are in your right senses; driving should even be the last. You don't need to hurry; after all, the car will be at your beck and call to drive it the way you want.

Note this, the wrong person comes with the intention to drive your body and not to love you, and when he is done with driving your body, he goes, looking for another body to drive. A reasonable person will study the features of the car before driving it. The truth is that if one is sane enough, he has to go through the proper procedure of purchasing a car. Reasonable person will, even when the car has been delivered in his house, take time to study the manual and so on and so fault, so as not to make a better use of the car properly and how to maintain it too. His main aim is not quenching that need for driving the car to work at that moment, but driving the car to other places and benefiting maximally from the luxuriousness of the car, and for the car to last long. Same with a relationship, it does not just serve a purpose; it serves multiple purposes so care should be taken in purchasing one.

Some have this wrong notion that romance will cement the relationship and make it superb. That is another fallacy; in fact, a pathological lie. It comes slowly when the person is for real. What if you didn't do the needful in learning more about the features of the car before driving it and at last you found out that the car has some features which you don't know how to use? Or the car may even lack some features you want? Will you then drive back to the company and demand for a refund or will you just dump the car in your garage and go for another good one? It is only the wrong person that will do so, to the detriment of others. How much more humans that are more complicated than car, how severely you or the other person will pay the price. You should keep alert as to know who is more serious in starting a relationship or starting with your body. Yes, some want to start with people's body and not a relationship. You might be thinking that you are in a relationship, whereas the other person is in a relationship with just your body. The right person wants more than just your body; the person wants something more special and not superficial. It is the features of a car that will make someone eager enough to purchase and drive a car, and enjoy the driving. If you don't learn about the features of the car how then will you make maximum use of the car? After all there lots of bodies out there, but something must have drawn the person to you and that shows is the right person. You don't even need to tell the person to take it easy when it comes to romance, the person

YES, ONLY TO THE RIGHT PERSON

will show you that romance is not that of utmost priority to him. He wants to learn more about you so as to enjoy the ride to the fullest.

Some will keep giving myopic excuses like; "I mean it is not a big deal lubricating the relationship with romance." But then, it proves that the person pushing the romance so fast just in few days or weeks of starting the relationship has no good intention about starting a lasting relationship. The funny thing is that the more the romance goes deeper, the more one person will get weaker and stupid to make proper assessment of the other person he wants to start a relationship with. Every good relationship has a reason, and that reason should not just be to satisfy your body. If that be the main reason for one going into a relationship, then danger is lurking around the corner. Humans are not like animals, that out of instincts they mate for just a reason, to continue the lineage. Relationship is meant to make people involved in it to be happy and not feel exploited.

Then when finally, that romance will come to manifest in the relationship, it will be gradually, and you will find out that it is done spontaneously out of love and not out of exploitation by one person selfishly exploiting the other. It is done out of mutual agreement, yielding to the workings of the body chemistry of both parties when serious commitment is made. No matter how superb you think that a relationship is, hot, early romance is never a characteristic of a real love but rather, a characteristic of exploitation perpetuated by one person, using romance as a weapon to hunt the other person down. So keep your eyes on the lookout as to when you will be preyed on by the wrong person enticing you with a fast romance. This person has a placard and that placard reads only but this: "I am a wrong person."

That right person comes with that real love delaying romance till the appropriate time. This person has the intention of wanting to make a future with you and not for you to make his bed. If one could be so mature enough to control his sexual feelings, then it says a lot about the person. He is such one that has self-control and not the sort that is being driven by feelings. Such a person is the kind you need in a relationship to make a great partner. He wants to build a relationship and not build on your body, loving you first and not laying you; and this love is built in the heart and not in the bed.

Quality 4

Time Makes It Stronger

"Time is a doctor, it cures; a magician, it tells of mystery; a talkative, it reveals the deepest secrets; a counselor, it gives advice; a teacher, it imparts knowledge. Most important, it's a light; it shines in the darkest place to make everything visible." - **O.D. Chimex.**

We live in a world where many regard time only with respect to its financial benefits. We are also conversant with this phrase: "That time solves every matter." I totally agree to these two schools of thoughts. Though a particular problem might not be curable, but time as well makes the sufferer to be dogged and resilient in dealing with such trouble. There is another school of thought that many people do not pay attention to, and that is: "Time plays a very big role in a relationship." This fact that time plays an important role in a relationship makes very few wise people to want to be longer in a relationship before making a commitment. They believe that with time lots will be revealed about the relationship. Though time plays the major part in the job, human effort is also needed in helping the time to achieve a better goal. Watchfully allowing a relationship to go through a test of time is one of the minor role humans can play. They do so to study the person, and that is their own contribution in this time solving job. But then, more to revealing a person's character is the role time plays in a relationship. It goes on to do other important jobs in a relationship which only time and not you, will do. Have you wondered how many times your patience paid off? This is because you were intelligent enough to allow a little time to pass, and you didn't regret it. That time you waited for something patiently, either made you to learn more, see areas to make amendment or gather experiences with which you improved on that thing. This same experience also will be beneficial to you if you allow some time to go on in your relationship, while you watch the wonders it will tell you. The longer the right relationship with the right person goes, the stronger it becomes. This time will make you to see not just what you want to see, but what you need to see. Time makes is possible for secrets to be revealed, and if yet you find basis to be in the relationship, then it is for real.

Some are very quick to fall head over in a relationship with someone so sudden, simple because they might be too inexperienced or just that they are yet to experience the benefits of patience. Maybe you have seen some of the little good qualities of the person and wow, this person is the best. Or that your own yardstick for a partner is met, you are like, "this person is just what I want." That is high point of naivety I call it. Few weeks, few months, are not enough to get to know one you are about to give the most delicate and fragile part of your body; which is, your heart. Not enough to conclude that the relationship is perfect. Even if they are enough, what about other things you need to know? Again going by that illustration of buying a car; you have walked into the motor company to purchase a vehicle. Remember this vehicle when you drive it, has your life at its fingertips. It can take your life or can as well enhance your life by adding an amount of comfort to your life. It goes on to take you to work, take you to places; in fact lessen the stress for you. The benefits are quite enormous and serious right? For these reasons you should not just pick out any flashy car in the showroom simply because it is at your disposal. Considering the fact that a serious

YES, ONLY TO THE RIGHT PERSON

issue which is your life if involved will make you to take your time to study the features of the car you want to buy. This process requires an amount of time to pass, say days. In some cases, a serious minded person will want to enlist other people's knowledge about that particular car. The same in a relationship; you have to give it a much longer time to get to know more about the features of this partner. Allow time to tell you more, and open your eyes to more things. And only a right relationship with the right person is made sweeter and stronger by time. A wise person understands that the relationship itself naturally needs time to show its characteristics. Allow it time to face a bit of challenges and obstacles and see if it will weather the storm. That time allowing process also makes your feelings to come to terms with reality and adjust automatically to these realities. It is only time that will tell whether that first impression you have for this person, or you have developed for this person is for real. If the relationship finds a basis to continue existing then only time will provide it with such basis.

It has often been noticed that in a relationship where the right persons are involved, love grows gradually with time like a mustard seed without either of them knowing, until it grows into a gigantic tree becoming a safe haven for both. Both of you need not to be told that time is making it so clear that the relationship is for real. When you are with the wrong person or in a wrong relationship, you find out that as time progresses, it becomes glaring that you both are not compatible or that the other person is the wrong person. The person's qualities will begin to manifest, the true feelings for this person also will be revealed. You might even find out that those surging feelings will on its own begin to go down as time goes on, and more reasons to end the relationship are given. Instead of saying "I love you; I'm madly falling for you," let time be the one to say those words and not you. And when it is time saying it, the relationship is for real.

People have taken time for granted; they have neglected this very important work that time does. They hastily and ignorantly go with their emotions thinking that every other thing will fall into place just within a very short time. That is a very big lie you are telling yourself, those warning signs, only time will tell you that. Why not allow time to go first while your emotions come at last; although it is always not too easy to put your emotions on checks. But then which one is harder, to spew those emotions to a crash? This statement should keep echoing in your heart that a patient dog eats the fattest bone. If you really want to go into a commitment in a relationship, you really need time to guide you and not your emotions to guide you. Time will only tell you if the relationship will go on or not.

Again remember, while you are allowing time to do its own job, your whole heart should not be involved, but your whole brain should be involved. Some people make the mistake of allowing their emotions to go before their brain and they tend to be stubborn or rather unaware to heed the advice that time will give them. Time will not do the work alone; you also have a part to play. This is why you have to work with time, and not passively watch while your emotions distract you, allowing time to do the job alone. What do I mean by this? I will tell a story of myself, a life story. When I was growing up, I goofed in the misnomer of this term that time settles every mater. Instead of putting efforts to become successful, I folded my hands waiting for time to work out perfectly to make me successful; that was a disaster. I hit late teen, still time has not solved my problem. Till I hit mid 20's reality dawned on me that in as much as time solves a problem that I have to also play a role in that time solving formula if I want a perfect solution. The same applies to relationship; time plays an advantageous role that is very important and should not be neglected. This will only be perfected when you are alert and cooperate with time when it will be telling you whether the relationship is good or bad. This important role requires efforts on your part too; it is a two way thing. In as much as time is working, you also should be working in tandem with time by being watchful enough to take the secrets time will be revealing to you,

YES, ONLY TO THE RIGHT PERSON

and take a step. How do you do this? You don't really have to fold your hands and fell head over in love, you have to keep at alert in examining these person's qualities and flaws which time will be divulging; weighing if it is really the kind of person you want to entrust your heart to. Do not just fold your arms dwelling on how wonderful you will be with this person simply because he has shown you a bit of what you want to see. There are other things you should see which only time will show you that if you allow it. Allow time to pass so as to study this particular person and make an honest observation. Wait for time to convince your emotions. While you allow time to pass, put your feelings and heart aside, while you work with your brain alone.

If you take your time to study, I mean do a thorough study on breakups and divorces; you will find out that most of them did not give time a place to play its role. Even if they did allow time, they did not work with time; they left the whole job to time while they were distracted by their emotions, allowing their emotions to make trivial the things that time divulged. Maybe, they weren't observant when time showed then what they needed to know. The reason for allowing your brain to work with time instead of emotions is that brain is a better judge than emotions. Emotions always give an ex parte judgment, but brain does not give a prima facie judgment, rather it does a whole lot of cross examinations before arriving at a judgment. Although age might be another factor in using both emotions and brain, but caution should be taken and efforts should be put in keeping emotions on check while you work with time. A relationship that can stand the test of time growing stronger without fading is always the one with the right persons who are in real love. This fact remains indubitable and cannot be underestimated. No matter how you might see it, time will always do the job of a magician, a talkative, a teacher, a counselor, and shining as a light in a relationship. It will tell you whether you need to be in the relationship or not.

Quality 5

Warns You of Danger

"She didn't need to understand the meaning of life; it was enough to find someone who did, and then fall asleep as a child sleeps, knowing that someone stronger than you is protecting you from all evil and danger."

- Paulo Coelho.

The first look at this title, one may begin to wonder how unintelligible it is. "I mean even your enemy will warn you of danger." This might be your conclusion, but then there is more to it. Have you thought about danger in disguise? Have you thought about dangers that come in a form of fun, camouflaging as something advantageous at the onset? There are dangerous things that look good at the onset, and gradually it will lead to doom. Those things are like fanciful tombs, seemingly good but filled with vile things. In other words, you could liken them to a kamikaze. It takes one with insight and real love for one to warn you of this and let you not do things that will harm you even if they might be pleasing to you. What does this statement mean? Someone might see his friend taking actions that are self-destructive although it is fun to him; yet he will allow that friend to enjoy to his death. Imagine when your friend does drugs, this is fun

YES, ONLY TO THE RIGHT PERSON

to such a friend, and you accept that way of having fun. You condone this friends' bad habit or shy away from telling him, just to avoid hurting this friend. This shows you don't love such person, because you will not allow your sibling to do such, because you really love such sibling very much. Kids do this a lot simply because of naivety, some adults do it too but out of lack of real love for such friend. Kids will see their friend indulging in destructive fun yet will desist from telling either the friend or the friend's parents. When you are in the right relationship with the right person, you find out that those sweet dangers; this one will not allow you do that.

I remember when we were in school, at elementary level; we used to engage in a very dangerous fun. This fun was performing acrobatics while on air. At first, one may see such as fun, but the risk is not what taking. And almost all the parents frowned at their kids doing this, yet we all tried as much as possible to hide this exuberant and risky fun from our parents. To us then, we were trustworthy friends and we got each other's back. Looking at it within our age brackets, we were loyal friends. That was a very serious mistake we made then, because as time went on, we began reaping the fruits of such stupid and fake love. Almost all of us got injured in one time of the other in the process of performing those acrobatics and hiding it from out parents. Some paid the high price, with morbidities. In fact one of us paid a very high price; he was amputated due to injury sustained from one of the failed attempts. Instead of us reporting to his parents then, we were again stupidly loyal and hid this secret, until the injury became worst and gangrened. Should we say that we showed love to ourselves? No, most of us would have ended up with such fate if not that our injuries were not severe and that it was noticed too early.

In some relationships, you find out that everything they do their partners take it with the mentality that so far as it makes them happy that they should continue doing it. Yes to such a wrong partner, you may do whatever you like to please yourself, and he supports you.

Maybe the person doesn't want to hurt that other person's feelings. But that is absolutely wrong; one that really loves you will not see a danger lurking disguisedly in your front and keep quiet. No matter how fun it will be to you, this right person will continue to make you see reason to change your course. He knows you will get hurt in the long run and that he will persist on letting you know. Now, is it the same in your case? If this person will not warn you of danger even though it might seem good to you at the onset, then this person may not really have that real love for you as he professes. A right relationship is one where both partners protect each other from not just seen dangers, but unseen dangers.

To buttress this fact, look at the love between parents and their children, sensible parents no matter how madly in love they have fallen with their kids, will never hesitate to correct or warn the child of that sweet danger. This should be the same with the person that professes love for you. That which you think might be fun, but will be disastrous in the near future should be brought to your notice, even if it will hurt you. Call it business or any other venture or lifestyle, even friends that you keep. In your career, in your choice of association, recreation, and hobby; these are likely where this disguised danger lies. One who professes love for you should take your interest at heart and always warn you of this disguised danger. You may not really know such is dangerous, but it takes one who sincerely cares about you and loves you to protect you from danger unseen. At first, your conclusion might be that this person actually does not want you to be happy, but really, he wants you to enjoy life without regret. Your safety should be this person's safety and your business should be this person's business. If this kind of warning and protection are lacking, then that love should be seriously examined. "Oh my dear, if this will make you happy, then I am happy too." That is a lie. The person is just not really interested in your business. The person is only interested in what happiness he is gaining from you at the moment – selfishness, I will call it. If it is that

YES, ONLY TO THE RIGHT PERSON

the person is really ignorant of that unseen danger, then the person is too busy to think about your welfare and safety. And if someone is too busy to pay attention to every little thing that happens in your life, tell me how the person will love you in every little way.

What if this person really does care and pay attention to your activities, but he is not smart enough to see those dangers in disguise? This shows that your life is at risk with such a person that has no insight to protect you when the need arises. This person will not get your back when it will be necessary. That undermines the quality of being a partner, or a supporter. Some of the things that happen to people are avoidable, but because they are not with that right person to tell them that, they become victims. Humans are handicap as a result of imperfection. This imperfection goes a long way to distort not just their thinking but blinds them too when it comes to trivial matters that might likely turn to serious matters. And if a person will make that partner who will at all times shield you from these invisible hands of imperfection, then you will rarely make mistake that will subtly hurt you. In the real sense, that should be the essence of having a partner, to protect you when you are unaware of danger.

Although this place does not insinuate stalking you and your activities, but every little thing you tell or feel, should be considered by a wonderful partner. Lots of stories have been told about people telling their so-called friends on social networking sites about their intended suicide, and surprisingly, in most of the cases those so-called friends joked about it and then the next thing being the person's death reported. Real love did not exist in such friendships. This is the time to weigh your relationship, new ones, about to start or existing relationships and see if this quality is lacking in such. A right person will always keep an eye on you to warn you of any danger to show really that he loves you. For a real love, it will be better to feel hurt and know and void that unseen danger, than to vaunt you to destruction, simply because he doesn't want to stop your fun. A right person is more interested in protecting you, and not cheering you to your doom, even if you will find such protection not funny. Though, not controlling you, but letting you know how you will get hurt with this fun if you insist. And that really shows you are in a relationship where two heads are better than one. You need a partner who has some moral guards and discipline, who is refined enough with policies imbedded in him to be able to prevent and protect you from falling into trap set by just your imperfect nature.

Quality 6

Being Generous

"One of the biggest challenges in relationship comes from the fact that most people enter a relationship in order to get something; they are trying to find someone who is going to make them feel good. In reality, the only way a relationship will last is if you see your relationship as a place that you go to give, and not a place that you go to take." - **Anthony Robbins.**

People tend to neglect the importance of this word generosity in life. It goes a long way to say a lot about a person. Generosity, one of the most important qualities needed in a relationship; not just in a relationship, but also needed to make the world a bit livable. Talking about being generous, most times it has often been proven that people with generous heart are kind and they tend to make better partners too. Yes because it takes kindness to feel empathy for people and then give in order to make less the person's problem. It also takes kindness to feel like contributing to someone's happiness by giving, not just materially also emotionally. And what else does a relationship want than to be ready to give to the other partner. When one is kind, the person shows this kindness by giving generously and not grudgingly at every given opportunity. This is one of the qualities a right person must exhibit. Being a spendthrift or a splurge is totally different from being generous. Generosity goes with when a need arises and an appropriate request made or implied, and then granted. Did you take note of these three words, need, request and granted? It takes only one with kind heart to grant a request that is borne out of an appropriate need. You might not really make the request, but you could imply it, then this person takes notice of these and comes to your rescue. Contrast it with splurging. You might not really need something and the person out of boisterousness spends with just three intentions, to impress either you or others, to show off, or to buy you off. This important quality is one of the signs of that right person, ready to give you all the times, without withholding from you.

Although giving might not really be due to one being in need, but the point here is that a generous person always senses you are in need and the person feels happy to bridge that lacuna. Some might think that this quality does not really matter that after all, that some are born miser by nature. That is far from the truth, if someone can be that miser not to think it is necessary to give you, then how do you think the person will as well give when it is necessary? Being generous goes in two ways, a person that is generous will not only give materially, the person can as well give emotionally. And it takes one with a generous heart to give emotionally as well. Come to think of it, if one is a scrooge, tell me why this person won't as well hoard emotional gifts? This generous person also will be ready to give you attention and time, because giving is in him. He will always want to give and share with you, no matter how small it is, this shows love.

Assuming the person has molded himself or circumstances has molded him into being a miser, but then traces of generosity will be visible when a need arises. And when an appropriate request is being made or visibly implied, the person must be moved to give support proportionate to the request, if he has the resources at the moment. This is a very important issue in weighing a potential right person for

YES, ONLY TO THE RIGHT PERSON

you. But it is sad that most people have played blind, deaf and dump in this regard. They think and reason, that after all, they have it materially, so in that case they don't bother about generosity. There they go wrong, very wrong. Even if you have a house filled with lots of candies, one who is really generous will still share a lollipop with you. That shows kindness on the person's part. The same way the person gives materially no matter how little and needless you might think it is, is the same way he will give emotionally and in other ways when the need arises. Economic situation might make some to look as if he is not generous, but then, one that is generous will always find a way to augment that which economic situation has made lacking. While you are busy falling in love do not neglect to access if the person really shows the willingness to give, whether in time, advice, materially, emotionally and otherwise.

It has often been noticed too that those who are not generous are somehow cold at heart and mean. When I was growing up, I used to have an uncle who will always boast how a scrooge he was, that he will have enough in his bank account and will not spend till a problem gets serious or goes out of hand. This means this person loves that material thing more than anyone, think really deep about this. This person is in another way saying, "To hell with you, I really need these material things more than you. So I prefer to keep them to myself than keeping you to myself." Pragmatically, if placed in the person's front, 'you and wealth' do not be surprised that he will choose wealth over you. But to be realistic, I don't think being a scrooge or not being generous is inborn, in fact it is out of nature. People just take in this, unknowingly, and allows it to grow in them. We were created in God's image and by virtue of that, we have in us those attributes of God, like love, generosity and the rest of them. God is really generous, looking around us seeing those endowments by nature that we enjoy, shows us how generous God is. And since we are made with qualities like his, we should as well exhibit generousness. If one can really spend a fortune on himself that means the person as well is generous just that he is too selfish; and that shows lack of love for others.

This is the time to take to heart this quality when searching for the right person. You may not really always ask or imply, but this generous person who really loves you will always assume that you need something and will be willing to give that. The person gives happily and not grudgingly or dutifully. Take note of these words, happily, grudgingly and dutifully. The person gives not because it is a duty to, but because it gives him joy to give you, no matter how little and in what form the giving comes. He also gives not because you have disturbed him for long, "Let me just give this to you so that you will stop disturbing my life." That is not his mindset. A generous person always gives not wanting anything in return and does not give when he will as well benefit in that. What else does a right relationship mean if not to go into it with the mindset of giving the other person and not receiving from the other person? Someone might be taking you out for a dinner, but the person does that because he benefits from that dinner too. What if the person gives you money to go take that dinner alone? Then it shows the person really gives from the heart.

In my vicinity it is rampant for people to take you out for a drink, lunch and so on and so forth, but then make that mistake of asking the person for financial support to solve one trouble or the other; the person will surprise you by giving you uncountable stupid reasons for not giving you that financial help. You might wonder is this not the same person that will always like to take you out and spend on whatever you may consume, but will not deem it necessary to help you out financially. There might be two possible reasons behind that, the person is just selfishly generous. First, he takes you out just because your company is good for him. Second, he wants to take lunch at that moment so he wants you to accompany him, let it be clear to others that he is paying your bills. Being truly generous differentiates one with kind of heart, which really is one of the attributes of the right person.

YES, ONLY TO THE RIGHT PERSON

The right person will always see a relationship as a place to go give and not to go get, unless the person is selfish. If two persons happen to have this mindset, each one with the purpose of giving, tell me why the relationship will not be such a sweet one. The more each person finds joy in giving to the other person, the more the joy they get. But if they hoard, then every other thing that relationship needs to grow will selfishly be hoarded. And this reminds me of two men that called themselves friends. They will travel in a car for like one thousand five hundred kilometers on a business trip, and will chose to be hungry. Simply because no one wants to buy lunch since the other person will request lunch too. In relationship, giving is the motive, and anything short of this, shows a selfish person. The more one gives in a relationship, the more happy that person will become and not by just receiving. This magic, only a generous person understands, and this generous person will likely make a good partner. This quality should be very visible in this person not just visible, but should be his way of life.

Quality 7

Being Altruistic

"Selflessness; it should be the basis of every relationship. If a person truly cares about you, they will get more pleasure from the way they make you feel, rather than the way you make them feel." - **Colleen Hoover.**

Could you remember the last time someone put your interest ahead of his? It happened recently, maybe from a family member, a close friend, or a relative; how moved you were that very day. This tells you how important this quality makes someone feel. Assuming this selflessness becomes a continuous occurrence, getting it from someone you are in a relationship with. Don't you think such relationship is bound to last? It should be the guiding principle in any relationship, in fact the foundation. Before discussing further on this quality, it will be appropriate to examine the dictionary meaning of this word, altruism. "It is defined as the selfless concern for the wellbeing of others. The Zoology meaning - behaviour of an animal that benefits another at its own expense. This is well stated, and in other words, it can as well be said to be unselfishness. This is one of those very vital qualities the right person possesses which every relationship needs. Sadly, this very quality is becoming rare in the world we live today, and relationship is not exempted. People tend to always show a, 'me-first' attitude and as a result of this, relationship has continued to fail. Most people go into relationship just for them to be selfishly satisfied. They tend to put themselves first before the relationship itself, thereby forgetting to show this wonderful quality. For a person to likely make a good partner, this quality must be visible in him, and it shows the person really comes to build a relationship.

This quality is very important in any relationship if it has to thrive and survive, and it is only when a person is for real and not fake that he manifests this rare quality. He is willing to show concern for your wellbeing; you are the first to be put into consideration in any matter. Before any decision or action is initiated, you will first be put into consideration, in order for you not to fare badly by such potential decision or action. This makes the person to always think of you first before himself. Do not be blinded by mere facade, be at alert to seek for this in a relationship; it is very important.

Some are confused by a mere display of deceitful actions by the partner: "He is so engrossed with me. Oh; she is so obsessed with me. He can't do without me, and she can't stay a minute without calling me on phone or texting me." Yes we know and we have quite heard that a number of times if not countless times. But look at those statements, the beneficiary of each of them has become just one of the partners. And that shows lack of altruism in that relationship. A selfless partner who really loves you will always think of your benefit in that relationship and not his. And no doubt if this partner lacks this quality, this relationship is one-sided; he is the one receiving, instead of giving. This person saying these might is the one getting all the satisfaction, and that shouldn't be.

One person cares not whether the other person gets as much happiness as he is getting. So engrossed in himself that he thinks he should always gain, and that is why such a partner feels and says how much he gains when with you. This act of selfishness always breaks relationships, and such partner always wanting to gain, shows a sign of being the wrong person. You can as well look at it this way; the reason for that obsession. This person always feel satisfied being with you and not bothered if you feel satisfied too being with him. What interests him is to feel happy with you and not to make you feel happy.

The truth is that real relationship should be based on the ability to impact positively on the life of each one involved, and that is to put the other person first. This a right person always has in mind, ready to give at all cost. The partner to the relationship should always have in mind to make you feel better and not to receive alone from you. The right person should always be seeking for an avenue to put a smile on your face even to his own detriment. That concern for your wellbeing should be visibly seen, it shouldn't be a verbal thing, and that is what selflessness takes into consideration. The receiver should always feel truly that this person shows genuine concern, by actions. Now take a look at these questions: "Please what time do you think will be best for you? Hope you enjoyed it? Do you need me to help you? How do you want it to be done?" These questions tell it all that a person is for real putting you first in the relationship. Your happiness, this person puts first and not his own happiness; and your wellbeing matters a lot and should be paramount to your partner. One who truly loves you does it this way, making you to be the beneficiary while he becomes the benefactor.

Looking at that zoology meaning of altruism – it shows that the behaviour must be to benefit the other person even at the expense of the benefactor. That is what the right person does, always ready to either sacrifice something or let go of something for your sake sake. I have read lots of stories and watched in movies about people dying for their loved ones, but I came to terms with the reality when a husband used himself as a human shield to protect his wife in a recent terrorist attack. It became glaring and more real to me that the spirit of altruism is diametrically defined in that single intrepid act. On no way will that same man treat his wife badly, not even in his dream. This man was willing to protect his wife even at the expense of his life, and this kind of spirit should be guiding any good relationship. Though everybody must not be that brave to express selflessness in that manner, but then the right person will always show that you are number one in his life. He always accepts to suffer the pain while you gain; he chooses to be the second while you are the first. The person's actions will say it better and not just his words. It is far better to show it than say it. At every given moment, the person's actions show that your wellbeing is very important to him; and anything short of this, the person is not for real. You should keep the search on for the person with such quality and not waste your time with the wrong person lacking this quality. Think of the trust you will have for this person, to always feel confident that you count first in this person's life.

How happy you will be to reciprocate that same spirit and take the relationship to a higher level. If two people in a relationship have this in mind and understand that both should always put the other person first, that starts the beginning of a union ready to achieve its purpose maximally.

To buttress this fact more, think of a mother breastfeeding a baby, though hungry, feeding the baby remains her priority even though she may be hungrier than the child. Just the cry of the baby, the looks and the discomfort the baby displays, make the mother to always abandon her own wish to serve the baby firstly. This depicts real love a mother has for her child. Do not be deceived by words, any person who professes love for you should be ready to put your interest ahead of his; it is nonnegotiable. He should act it and not say it. Do not be hoodwinked by thinking that the person's obsession being with you shows he is madly in love with you. The person is just selfish, trying to get happiness from being around you and not trying to give you happiness by his presence. The right person will always ask if you would like you both to meet and not mandating you to meet him with that camouflage that your presence makes him happy. How much happy you are when with him should be his priority and not how much happy he is while you are with him. The handwriting is always on the wall if you are vigilant enough to study the person you are starting a relationship with, or the person that you have been in a relationship with. Do not neglect this important quality; it is only the right person that will exhibit such.

Although, infatuation is always disguising, confusing some to believe that it is real love, whereas it is not. To this person, you, and not him should come first, and it is only one with real love that will be willing to show this attitude toward you all the time. You will feel the person putting you first without him knowing that he does such. Selflessness is natural when the right person shows it, making the relationship to be a place to go give and not a place to go get. And if this is well understood by the parties, bonding becomes stronger and happiness of both becomes plenty. The more altruistic your partner is in the relationship, the more secure the relationship will be. The same way the less of this quality from a partner, the more vulnerable and dangerous the relationship will be, exploiting you.

Quality 8

Does Not Keep A Count of Wrongs

"When you stop expecting people to be perfect, you can love them for who they are." - **Donald Miller***.*

"I'm counting it for you, and time will come when I won't take it any longer. This is the second time you are doing this; I guess third time will not be funny." Have you heard someone say something similar to this? Though it might not really be said exactly this way, but the tone of the voice will all point to one thing; that the person is not forgiving your errors. "Hey, I don't really like what you have just done to me. Hey, this attitude just pisses me off." How do these statements sound? Simple and sympathetic right? That is exactly how one who truly loves complains about being hurt and not going on and on blabbing about how many times you have gone wrong and how many times left for you not to be forgiven. When one truly loves, he has no need keeping account of injury or things you have done wrong in the past. Past is past, what matters is the future, only the right person understands this. There is this proverb in my locality that I have always proved wrong and I hate to quote it. It says: "Not the day a child mistakenly pours out a gallon of oil that the child is punished." Could you beat that, does it not show bearing grudge? Imagine when your child does something wrong and you mark it on a calendar waiting till the wrong has become so bad then, the punishment would be borne out of accumulated wrongs and anger. One who loves you does not count how many times you have wronged but how many times you have righted.

Though sometimes we might mistakenly mention what wrong someone has done us in the past, but that could be as a result of imperfection that we say that. It becomes risky when it is a habit to keep reciting the past wrongs whenever the new wrong is done. The right person for you will try as much as possible not to remember the wrong of the past, in fact the person unknowingly forgets due to intense real love the person has for you. Be careful not take this quality with triviality; it matters a lot and only the one that really loves you will exhibit this rare quality. Ask yourself if this person keeps recording account of the injury in the past, how will he not harm you in the near future when he thinks that your wrongs have climaxed, therefore unforgivable? Imagine you are keeping a heap of dirty clothes, maybe you lack the time to wash them. At some extent, the heap of dirty clothes will accumulate that you will be forced to act decisively upon it. The same way when one keeps recording wrong and doesn't forget, it will get to an extent that the person will be pushed to act rashly. Should a relationship be like this? The answer is no, and will continue to be a no answer. In a relationship, it is not meant to be like human law where you go in for any serious wrong you committed. No matter how bad the wrong is, that right person will always have a basis to forgive you and never to bring it to haunt you in the near future so far as you are willing to turn a new leaf. Of what benefit will it be for him, to continue to remember your wrongs when he knows you are too wonderful and that your good has covered for your bad?

Remember there is a great difference between forgiving and forgetting, but the two should always work in pari-passu if this person is for real. The right person will forgive as well as forget that wrong, in the sense that you will never be again judged with that wrongs forgiven.

YES, ONLY TO THE RIGHT PERSON

One who fakes love will though forgive, but will not forget, the wrong is recorded actually in a logbook waiting for the appropriate time to act upon it. "This is the second time, you are doing this." Be very careful if this becomes a continuous occurrence in your relationship. It is a warning sign that the person might be vindictive. Though he may profess love for you, but then it is just not for real. Yes, this person really is the wrong person to be with; revenge will always be the order of the day, if care is not taken. Then if that be the case, does it not show you that such person is really not in love with you? Don't you think your life will be endangered since you know that you will not always escape mistake? One with real love comes with a spirit of not counting how many times you have wronged, but how many times you do something spectacular will always be remembered. Even the bible states that love does not keep account of injury. So why not take into account this quality that is a very important ingredient of real love so as to weigh this partner? Keep wronging the person; he will lovingly keep correcting you without feeling it is time to pay you back. Enough will not be enough, so far as you keep working so hard to do the right thing, and not purposely making the same mistake often.

I will tell this wonderful story of a temple boy; though I watched it in a movie. A temple boy very tender was working with a much older master in the temple. The boy will always do wrong and will always cry to the temple master with fear that he will be severely punished. But then, he was wrong. Each time he wronged, the temple master will lovingly tell him: "Just say the word, I'm sorry." And the boy will happily go back to his duty post. As how many times he wronged the master, he always came back and said those words to his master: "I'm sorry." And there he went free. One hot afternoon, the temple master was in the temple's den performing a ritual, when the boy mistakenly pushed down the lamp hung at the entrance of the temple when he was rushing out to carry out one of his duties. Unbeknownst to him that the lamp had ignited the temple curtain, he picked it up and stood it and went his way. By the time he could return back to his master to say sorry about the lamp he mistakenly pushed down and to report the errand he sent him, the whole temple has been raised down to ashes including his master who was inside praying. And this boy will never forget the exceptional love shown to him by his master who was ready to bear the brunt than let him bear it. One who loves you will not mind to suffer as a result of your mistake, instead of subjecting you to that suffer because of your mistake.

Though one should not condone stupidity, but the fact remains that, one who willingly accepts those words: "I'm sorry when being wronged, is actually a right one, he accepts you have weak points and that you are eager to improve. And like that temple master too, he does not and will never count how many times he has been wronged. Like it has been mentioned earlier, the better way to know one who does not count wrong is by the person's utterances. Vigilance is needed on your part to analyze the utterances of the person and the gestures when wronged. It is not necessary to wantonly wrong a person to see the person's reaction; your imperfection will always push you to; and when such happens, the person's reaction will show if he counts the wrong or not. Character is always like pregnancy and will not take time before it becomes glaring. The right person will never and does not keep account of wrongs no matter how much and how far you have defaulted in the past. This will tell you that you are loved with your flaws. How wonderful you will feel and grateful you will be moved to love back the one that loves you that way. And this is like a chain reaction making the relationship to move to greater heights. How you will be forced to keep account of the person's own wrong to nail him too as revenge, if such a person counts your wrongs too. The outcome of this, being a relationship with two people, ready to get at each other most of the times.

"An eye for an eye only ends up making the whole world blind." Mahatma Gandhi. And you will not want to go into a relationship where

YES, ONLY TO THE RIGHT PERSON

you both will end up being blind in the name of revenging each other. If that be the case, no other result than plunging the relationship into a ditch; that becomes the end of it. Someone who loves you and is likely going to make a right partner will not be counting your wrongs, so far as you are putting efforts not to repeat same mistake often.

Quality 9

Letting Your Opinion Count

"The greatest compliment that was ever paid me was when someone asked me what I thought, and attended to my answer." - **Henry David Thoreau.**

You might not know how it hurts until someone constantly ignores your opinion, especially one very close to you. But how happy and fulfilled you will be when someone always puts your opinion into consideration, you will feel a great sense of belonging. This is a very essential and another significant quality of being in the right relationship with the right person; no doubt about that. And it can as well be easily noticed when one's opinion or viewpoint counts in a relationship. Although in some cultures, it has made it practically not important in a relationship, but in the actual sense it is very essential. If you are not being considered while making even the minutest decision, tell me how you would be considered when weightier decisions are made? Some people might think that it only concerns women, but it does not; the men too are concerned in this regard. Assuming you are in a relationship and you don't know about anything until it happens. For instance, your partner tells you something only after it has been done. You keep getting the lies that he wants to surprise you, whereas it is just the person not interested in your opinion. For the fact that you

YES, ONLY TO THE RIGHT PERSON

are in a relationship, your view should always not just be sort, but when it is necessary should be considered. You should always have a say in matters. Some in relationship will try to deceive their partners by just seeking their opinion in few certain things, and not trying as much as possible to bring a synergy with such opinions. Their reason for such is for seeking sake, and that is where it ends.

Seeking a partner's opinion and allowing it to form part of a decision when necessary does two things in a relationship, it shows that the relationship is not just a 'one-man show', but two men show, who want to make a collective decision for the good of the relationships. It shows that this person values you a lot to let your opinion count. Second, it gives you a sense of belonging and motivates you to always think of ideas to give out for the good of the relationship or the other person, when the need arises. In fact, when your opinion is sought in matters, and is allowed to count when necessary, this partner is invariable giving you a responsibility making you not to be dormant in such relationship. It is love that he will acknowledge that your view is important and should be considered, you should not be sidetracked. It is so funny that in democratic states, lots of military regimes take place in relationships. People profess that they are practicing advanced democracy but in the smallest units like relationship, they practice unitary system if not tyranny. Imagine when your partner wants to purchase a particular item and wants you to say what you feel like on that purchase. And how happy you will be when such partner makes necessary adjustments to accommodate those reasonable views of yours. Does that not show real love? This quality, only the right person will show.

Most times, it is done unknowingly but then, the right person will always want to seek for your opinion, I mean the person knows you are priceless so does your views. A partner allowing your viewpoint to count makes you happy and also ready to contribute when the need arises. Going by creation, God gave us that right to choose and not lording it over us just like animals are created with instincts. In essence, God is showing us by love that, 'look, you are important.' This very important aspect is needed in a relationship and one should always look out if such quality is noticeably visible in a partner. And if it is seriously lacking, that partner is found wanting. I am afraid; the person might not be that right person to give your heart to. How do think that you can cope with one who will like to manage you and your feelings like money, investing it only when it will be to his advantage? Then undermining the complexity and sophistication of such feelings. How will you cope with a person that thinks you don't matter? This is where you really need to take notice and not to look at it as a trivial matter. That your views are considered in all matters shows that you really are with a partner whose aim is to walk with you side by side to achieve the best of goals in unison.

Someone who doesn't take your opinion into consideration is indirectly telling you: "Look, you are worthless. I am the boss and should always do it alone." I have seen relationships and marriages that have run into deep troubles because this quality is lacking. And the victim goes in retaliation, hoarding very vital information that will be advantageous, simply because the person's opinion has been neglected and the person wants the other to fail so as to show how stupid his decisions are. Instead of working together to achieve a single goal, they become political parties laying in ambush to expose each other's flaws. One who loves you, I mean the right person with genuine love will try as much as possible to bring you into everything he does. You will not be excluded and kept in the dark. You will not be a dormant partner, but an active partner. When you have this feeling that your opinions are needed and that you are considered, you will as well try as much as possible to always have meaningful opinions to contribute in the relationship. With this mindset, when decisions fail, you both take responsibility, and not shifting the blame to one person.

YES, ONLY TO THE RIGHT PERSON

Allowing the opinion of the other person to count in a relationship is another way to show that such person is humble and down to earth. It is only a humble person that considers others' opinion. And this aspect of humility helps a relationship to thrive, everyone is always carried along. No matter how stupid an opinion is, there must be something to pick out of such opinion. And this is the reason wise people will always say, that even when a mentally retarded person is talking, you should first of all listen, before casting aspersions. Recently media has been inundated with this phrase: "Equality of sexes," this is as a result of people thinking that one sex is inferior; therefore their opinion should be kept in the backyard. In relationship, everybody's opinion counts and should be taken seriously into consideration, unless there is a very strong reason not to do so. This quality does not rule out privacy, but then, it only limits privacy in a relationship working towards an openness and equality which will invariable cement the relationship and solidify it. You need a partner who will always put your views into considerations at all time. A partner who will show you that you are priceless; and you need a partner who is ready to always make you feel that the relationship is resting on you, to either succeed or fail. And this quality most relationships lack, and watch out, those that lack it are heading to doom. One person will, instead of being a partner, will be a sufferer relegated to the background. If that becomes the case, how will he expect you to work as a partner when he implicitly tells you that he needs not your views?

Some people who are in relationships, when drastic and decisive decisions are needed, they will say: "I don't know, whichever way you want it, let it be so." This person has been made to be just an observer and not a partaker; one person has made the other to think less of himself. A relationship should always be two people working together to bring a synergy and not one person usurping the whole show thinking that he is superior to the other person. If you are not allowed to contribute, then how will you prove that you are a partner? If your opinion counts in a relationship, then your feelings will always count and you will always count as well. You will have in mind that it behoves you to make a positive impact on the other person or the relationship. You feel a sense of responsibility, and will want to deliver a good result. This way, you will be allowed to be a major shareholder in that relationship.

Quality 10

Doesn't Pay Attention to Your Flaws

"By nature, I know that I'm guiltier than you are; so why should I accuse you when I profess that I love you." -
O.D. Chimex.

You might be wondering how possible it is not to notice a person's flaws. Noticing a flaw is different from paying attention to it. When you pay attention to something, you start giving that thing a special attention or consideration so as to act toward it. For the fact that we all are imperfect, it means that as a matter of fact we are programmed with flaws, but not everybody understands this. People tend to forget, and go on with their actions to make others look error-filled, and themselves, without fault. How unreasonable for a kettle to call a pot, black. But then, how loving and beautiful it is when someone loves you, ignoring your flaws. It is only when you are in the right relationship with the right person that this will be possible. Though mistakes may be the order of the day, the right person will not always be taking into consideration those flaws in order to put it to your face that you really are always at fault. This person, though seeing your faults, will lovingly be playing blind to those faults of yours. The reason is that he knows really and thinks that your good side is far better to cover for your bad side. Even when the flaws become glaring, he lovingly corrects you and not condemning you for those flaws. Imagine the happiness, the joy and the confidence you will have knowing that someone is interested in you and not your mistakes. This shows reasonableness on the part of the person, as well as showing that he is such one to build a relationship with.

Most people, especially those ones that might make wrong partners, always ignore this important quality, putting other people's fault to them all the time. They see themselves as saints while seeing others as criminals, and that is because the love is lacking in the actual sense. If one professes love for another, why should he be too quick to paint that one as evil, knowing that he too is guilty of the offence? If one loves you, why should he be paying attention to your flaws all the time? One that will make a good partner will see no cause to think that he is better than you are, since everybody makes mistakes one time or the other. For the fact that the person sees your flaws and still not hammer on it, shows that he is accommodative; and a good relationship needs a partner that is accommodative. I mean what else do you need in a person than someone who understands you? You may be weird but this person understands and still does not pay attention to those funny sides of you so far as it is not too important. He looks at your good side and not at your flaws. This quality makes you to be ready to take gentle correction from such loving partner, because you see him as one who complements you. I could remember one of my lecturers in my university days; this woman was so sarcastic and impatient with students, and that was her way of life. Asking her question after lecture is like incurring her wrath; you are in essence telling her to tongue lash you. She lost her temper at every single minute. Almost every student was agitating that she should be demoted. I will never forget the day I became a direct victim to her hot-temper. I walked out of her office humiliated; I went to her office to report about her course I had double results in, maybe due to printing error. That very day, I concluded that this woman will not have a happy home. But I was wrong, fortunately I

YES, ONLY TO THE RIGHT PERSON

met someone in the same neighborhood with her and the person confessed she had a very caring and the most amazing man as husband, and both tend to cohabit well and peacefully. You see, her husband understands her and does not count her flaws, because she will always be losing her temper at her husband. If her husband had been a sort that takes this flaw of hers to notice, I wonder if they would have been couple. So if one really loves you, those minor flaws that are as a result of imperfection will not be taken seriously.

Sometimes this partner could get pissed off with this your attitude, but then love covers multitude of your sins. The pissing off is also as a result of his own imperfect nature; but then he does not go on to harp on the flaw making you look error-filled. Where there is wrong, love will see right and lovingly tries to correct that. If everybody's flaws are made glaring publicly, then we all could hide in shame and try not to make others look more criminal than us. This, the right person acknowledges and puts your flaws away. Even when it becomes obvious that you really have done it again the bad way, it will not make him to harmer on that flaws so as to put you down. This person's effort will concentrate on seeing you improve, and he has confidence that you will improve; and not dissipating it making you look lesser because of your flaws. Why should this person harmer on your flaws if he is the right person? He has no reason to lay ambush, for you to make mistake then he attacks you. People who are quick to point at others' fault always make bad partner, they will always be complaining at every little thing. This complain will only take away the peace of mind in such relationship, and nobody wants such relationship.

He is busy with making you a refined gold and not making your flaws stand out. He doesn't really have that time to keep at alert to point out your flaws; you give this person joy and not sadness. And that is how it is when you are with the right partner. Someone without this wonderful quality is not difficult to find out. To assess this partner, think how often he makes you feel that you are wrong? You can't remember the last time, right? And how often does he praise you for what good you have done? Almost all the time. Then this person has this wonderful quality that is very important in a partner. When you thought of that wrong you have done how serious it was, in fear you thought he will shout on you, only for him to calmly correct you. Does this not show you that he will likely make a wonderful partner? This is the reason loving parents don't always put their children's fault at them, rather they lovingly corrects them. And those kids will in turn love them to the extent of avoiding mistakes that will hurt them.

This person is equally telling you: "Look with all these flaws, I really love you. In fact I don't really see those flaws, rather I see those superb you." What a wonderful quality that every relationship needs. Now take for instance, you always want a sports car, your salary is like two thousand dollars a month; you know this is meager. You have come to reality that it might take you like your entire salary for life to purchase this sports car. Then one day, you were offered a Bugatti Veyron without you paying a dime. Do you think that you will reject this mouth-watering offer because this sports car has some minor electrical faults? Hell no, you will never think of those electrical faults, because you really know that the gift is priceless and that it is beyond your reach. This is exactly the way this wonderful person sees you. You should be that Bugatti that will cost him his salary all his life time, with minor electrical faults that would not inhibit the usage of the car.

Let you be that priceless to the person that your flaws will only be secondary to loving you. He knows that it is far cheaper to repair those minor electrical faults than losing that wonderful priceless gift which is you. He may even accept to drive the car with such little faults, not minding. He might as well be ready if it will cost him a year salary to repair the fault; he is still on a profit side any of the options he chooses. In a relationship, you need someone that knows your flaws and still yet, puts you above the flaws. You should want someone that is ready to correct your flaw and not to discard you because of the flaw. And if a

YES, ONLY TO THE RIGHT PERSON

person is willing to accommodate your flaw, you are home and dry, and your relationship is bound to grow. For the fact that those faults should not be made to stand out, tells you that you worth more than those flaws to this right person.

Quality 11

Settles Disagreement in a Short Time

"Fight is inevitable because we are different; misunderstanding is always, because we are humans; but understanding binds us together because we love each other." - **O.D. Chimex.**

You may have disagreed with your loving parents a few number of times. But the fastness in settling the disagreement and the efforts on both parties to forestall occurrence shows one thing, love. Disagreement is insidious to any relationship, due to its corrosive effects. The lesser it becomes in a relationship and the quicker any disagreement is settled, the more glaring it becomes that the parties are going to make right partners. If this partner is willing to settle any disagreement in a shortest period, then he is likely the right person. Constant occurrence of disagreement without being settled in a short time tends to eat a relationship gradually without people in it knowing. Due to our genetic makeup, upbringing, background, social and educational status, people in relationship always disagree sometimes. But the ability to put these impediments behind them and settle disagreements as soon as possible, amicably makes them compatible. Often, you hear of the word compatibility, it doesn't mean lack of disagreement in a relationship. It means lack of lingering disagreement

YES, ONLY TO THE RIGHT PERSON

and this shows a good relationship. This attribute is one of the ways to find out if the person actually is the right person for you. Is this partner a type that will always want a disagreement to be settled quickly? Do not take it for granted thinking it is not important. The right one who really loves you, will at all-times, be in the front burner to the settling of disagreement irrespective of whoever wronged first. This person shows that willing attitude to make matters right at all-times. The reason behind this is simple, it shows he is a peace loving person and will do everything to let the relationship grow and not to tear it down.

In some relationships, some partners do allow every disagreement to die down without settling it. Their reason is simple; they think that compatibility means pushing aside issues, but it is not. Settling a disagreement is not just allowing a quarrel to die down, but to discuss why, who and how, in order to forestall future occurrence. It is more reasonable to know that an issue exists and that it should be discussed; instead of acting as if nothing happens. This is not a movie; it is a real life situation and should be treated as one. If a disagreement comes up, which is expected of people with different ideologies, reality demands that it should be discussed and settled holistically. Someone with this mindset always makes a better partner. Some in relationship think that they are with the right person when this person is the kind that when any disagreement occurs and you call him to settle it, he says: "It's ok, it's in the past." And you think the person is a peace loving person? I don't think so, the person is that sort that doesn't settle disagreement, but pushes it beneath the carpet waiting for an appropriate time to dig it up. If someone sweeps issues away just like that, how then will future occurrence be forestalled? One with this right attitude to settling disagreements understands the realities in relationship and moves to correct it. No need to fake it like the characters always portrayed in movies, it should be faced, discussed and settled. It is such real person with this attitude that relationship needs to grow with.

Coming first and the willingness to make peace says it all, the person is not only a peace-loving person, but the person is also, humble; and these are the qualities you really need in someone whom you want to entrust with that delicate part of you which is the heart. What else do you want than someone who is ready all the time to make things work and not to tear things down. This person is always ready to build not only the relationship, but to build you too. Disagreement is like rust, it may look small at first but if left as unimportant, as time progresses, it builds up and eventually destroys a piece of metal. The quicker a disagreement is settled, the lesser time it is not allowed to metamorphosed to grudge. Settling of this disagreement is a mutual thing and not merely saying: "ok let's forget about what has happened." It is about saying: "Ok, how do we avoid this occurring in the future time?" A real settlement and not a fake settlement.

In some relationships, disagreements are allowed to linger and then turn into grudge and malice. I am afraid, if the person you are dating or about to start a relationship with is not the type that wants disagreement to be settled totally as soon as possible, then you need to have a rethink. Settlement of disagreement like mentioned earlier goes beyond just saying a mere word 'sorry.' It is not about settling a disagreement with a hug or a kiss. It is about sitting down to discuss in details what brought the disagreement and how each one has contributed to the escalation, then making the needed apology and corrections. A person with this ability to settle disagreement in a short time is invariably telling you: "Look we are different though, but our differences will not be a cause for concern in our relationship." He is also in essence telling you: "Our relationship will thrive even when the going gets though." And this is the kind of person you need to be in a relationship with. Not some sort of wrong person that will always not care if disagreement is settled or not.

Allowing a disagreement to die down and not talking it is like taking painkillers when you have a fractured bone. The painkiller might

YES, ONLY TO THE RIGHT PERSON

at the moment reduce the pain, but then the bone is getting damaged. The other way sitting down with an orthopedic surgeon, discussing your fracture with him and seeking a real treatment, heals the fractured bone. That is the same way you will find out that those things causing such disagreement will be treated totally and overcome sooner. You both will begin to understand each other better, avoiding things that will cause altercation and in the long run becoming more compatible. The more this person is ever ready to talk things out at the quickest time, the more he tells you that you both are studying yourselves to better understand ways to deal with each other without having issues. He makes you to understand that a perfect relationship is not one without issues but one with the people involved having that willingness and enthusiasm to settle those issues as soon as possible. For the fact that this person always wants disagreement to be talked out shows in essence that he as well will like every trouble to be talked out and not to be grudged upon. Imagine you were a mother and your daughter did something wrong, you scolded her and this girl not only apologized for being sorry went further to approach you at your most convenient time to discuss the issue with you. That child proved to be a good and intelligent child; not only will you also apologize for your rashness that moment, you will also lovingly correct that child making her avoid such mistake next time. On your path too, she may have pointed where you overreacted too, and that paves way for improvement. This will cement the bond between you and your daughter. The more this person shows that willingness to talk issues out, the more you have no cause to be angry unnecessarily with such person.

There is another good thing about a person that will always want disagreement to be discussed and settled in a short time. The more the avenue to dialogue, the more the bond between you both is becoming stronger. No matter what, you are very assured that he will never act because of grudge, since every matter always gets settled. You won't even have guilty conscience toward this person because you know very well that you have no unsettled business with him. Settling disagreement quickly goes a long way to make you both bare your heart and feelings to each other at every little disagreement, thereby seeing how you both feel about a disagreement. This quality, a right person displays to always make the relationship work at all time. Disagreement is somehow good in a relationship because it exposes the relationship, making the right partners to come together in charting a course. Not just that you both agree on everything, what about where you don't agree. That is where disagreement plays a part exposing and subjecting the relationship to test. But the wrong person will always tell you: "Please let us not settle this disagreement so that I could see reasons to leave you when the time comes."

Quality 12

Being Submissive

> *"Submission is not about authority and it is not just obedience; it is all about relationship of love and respect."*
> *- Wm. Paul Young.*

The media, civil right activists, and crusaders indirectly continue to make this wonderful quality to go into extinction. They always do this by their campaign for equal rights of the sexes, which indirectly pushes submission off relationship. But how ironical it is to notice that those campaigners always submit to superior authority. This is another quality that endears a whole lot of people to others, especially a particular sex to the other in a relationship. This particular quality is assumed to be expected mostly in women who will likely make a wonderful partner, although men should show a similar one, which is yielding. Being submissive does not really connote stupidity or subservience; in fact it goes a long way to tell more of how strong a person is. This very wonderful quality tends to endear a woman to a man and imparts really on any relationship. So one in a relationship gets to be enthralled when the other partner possesses this wonderful quality. It shows really that this one can be very accommodative and will always obey meekly when the rules are within the boundary. Only the right person will be willing to be submissive.

This also goes a long way to say how passive flexible one can be in a relationship, especially when issues arise. These issues are the kind that if not checkmated, could put a relationship on fire. But this submissive person has seen this even before hand and then out of rationality, goes a long way to allow what happens to happen. Not really that this person doesn't know what to do, or that she is powerless, but her insight and wisdom has made her to allow some certain things to happen for peace sake in a relationship. And this is very important in a relationship. If everybody assumes captainship, then who will fly this plane called relationship? Two pilots are always in the cockpit, but only one is allowed at every point in time to fly the plane. The other person could be a helper at each moment making this journey a smooth one. Though as the case may be, the pilots could be allowed to swap, only on a certain situation, when necessary.

This is exactly the same when it comes to relationship, though there are two pilots, one must be allowed to fly the plane while the other supports. And if one lacks submissiveness then how would you expect such plane to be safe? They are bound to land the plane to a descent. The same way they will crash the relationship, if the two people involve continue to assume heads at all times. One with this attribute tends to be a perfect supporter, that right partner, always augmenting the other person so as to allow this relationship to blossom. If this attribute is lacking in her, then there is danger lurking round the corner, sooner or later it will come out to attack the relationship. One with this quality does not mean that the person should be dull, or low in knowledge or experience. She might have all the smartness, be knowledgeable, and very experienced; yet she tends to exhibit this wonderful character just to make a relationship work, going by the rule. And that rule is that in any joint task, there must be a coordinator, heading the team; and this, this submissive person simply understands. She submits because she loves her partner, and she is for real.

YES, ONLY TO THE RIGHT PERSON

Most people belong to organizations and groups, and these organizations and groups have either a head or heads selected to take the lead. This does not really mean that those heads are perfectly or totally better than other members. Not at all, but for the sake of progress and avoiding topsy-turvy, they allow the heads to lead. So in a relationship as well, where two different persons are working together to achieve a particular goal, one person must be the head. This other person must also be submissive to the head so as to achieve that particular goal. This is not a duty; it comes from within to prove that it is not just a mere dutiful obligation. One that is submissive is always very intelligent to always avert situations that will cause a wreck to the relationship. She respects and loves the one having the mantle of leadership, for both to achieve that goal of a successful relationship. Not just respect and love, this right person supports the other to succeed in that job. Not only that she respects, loves, and supports, she also allows and accepts what happens or any right thing the other person does for the journey to be smooth and sweet. And when necessary, she gives the correction and advice humbly with regards to respecting the head pilot.

In some parts of the world, they always harp on the need for equality in everything, including relationship, indirectly saying that submissiveness should be out of the way. But they tend to contradict or rather obfuscate this by not making it clear to people that the equality should only be restricted to treatment and opportunities. This very important quality is needed in a partner especially the woman for a relationship to be a successful one. This submissive person knows and believes that there must be a leader when two or more persons are working together to achieve a particular goal, and relationship inclusive.

Financial status, political status, social status and academic status; these, this submissive person defiles to make a relationship work. I once read about a very wealthy woman, so wealthy that she could employ her husband as her driver if she wished to. Lots of people thought her husband would only be turned to an errand boy, thereby bringing the marriage to ruin; that was a lie. She had a very successful family with grown up kids, a wonderful man who stayed in charge and looked the boss. During that interview, the interviewer asked her the secret of her still happily married despite her economic and social status. Her answer was enthralling, she said and I quote her: "I still see my husband as the head of the family and submit to his authority. I wash his clothes and makes his food." And that says it all, her husband continues to love and cherish her allowing their relationship to thrive amidst distractions. This goes a long way to show the importance of this wonderful quality in a relationship. If she shows such quality, you need not to be worried what manner of partner she will make in a relationship. Only the right person will exhibit this sterling quality irrespective of her status in the society.

As stated previously, submissiveness is very different from stupidity; do not confuse them. Both are very far from each other. One who is submissive has it all, yet she allows for some certain things to happen, respecting the authority that should be. This right person will make you as her partner, be at peace. You don't really need to shout down the roof before things are done, and you will always be happy to relinquish or delegate assignment since you are comfortable that she will not usurp your position. No nagging, no constant and baseless arguments and no repetition and warning. These are some of the benefits you will have when she is such a submissive person. And only the right person will be submissive.

Imagine when this person is not submissive, not only that you will keep shouting over little things; you will be afraid not to be coup at any given moment. One might look good, but lacking this quality makes such one likely to be a wrong person to be in a relationship with. Imagine that moment you will constantly battle to make this person understand that there must be a head pilot. This person not submissive will be like struggling with you in the cockpit, and what do you expect

YES, ONLY TO THE RIGHT PERSON

to happen to the plane? This keeps destroying relationship, but some don't see is as very important thing in a relationship. If she constantly persists that it must always be done her way, then you are likely having a wrong partner with you. Out of love, she would willingly allow a relationship to have someone who takes the lead. And it is only love that will make a person to submit to a partner who takes the lead in a relationship. That a person says yes to all you say, does not make such person submissive, her actions and words after such yes is said will say more about how true that yes is. Only someone who possesses the qualities of a right person will say that yes with words and actions in tandem to back it up.

Quality 13

Being Humorous

"I don't trust anyone who doesn't laugh."
- Maya Angelou.

The moment I read Maya Angelou's quotation I burst into laughter. Though some people that seldom laughing might be exceptional, but the emphasis is on being jovial. It goes a long a way to say more of a person's heart, what a person is inside. Someone whose hobby is not just laughing but also making others laugh, becomes the one to be trusted more. Most times too, this quality of being humorous affects relationships in such a great way. One might really be thinking how on earth this quality makes a good partner. It is a quality that when you have a partner that possesses it, you are home and dry to making a good relationship with this person, as well as making the relationship more fun to be in. A lot of people will always crave to have a partner who will always make them laugh all the time, either by words or by action. And these abilities, humorous person possesses; such ones might be in for double reward. Few may think that someone that is humorous is always not serious and doesn't take life seriously. That is a fallacy; though humorous people tend to cross boundaries sometimes, but that does not mean that they are all that unserious all the time. There is more to what humorousness can do in a relationship instead of just making a

YES, ONLY TO THE RIGHT PERSON

partner laugh; it adds to relationship making it better than not. A person with this ability will likely make a good partner more than a person that is not. The reason for this conclusion is based on few concrete facts observed. I took my time to study lots of humorous people in my locality, especially comedians, and I found out that a greater number of them that are married stayed married. Then when you compare them with their showbiz counterpart like musicians and actors, you will see a great discrepancy. If you are still in doubt, you might also do your own search, and the result will always baffle you. How wonderful a humorous person can be, which will be brought to bear in a relationship. One with this quality is likely to make a wonderful partner in a relationship.

This quality adds a lot to making one a potential right person or not in a relationship. Someone who is very humorous always tends to be happy and takes matters not too serious. To such a person, you too can as well be joking always, if you make it look so. One like this, does not get angry easily; forgets and forgives easily too. What else do you want from a partner than someone who is ready to forgive and forget easily? This reminds me of a classmate that tends to joke all the time. You can make him angry, but tell him that you were joking; then he forgets. Even if you don't make the first move to apologize, he might find a way to joke about you and that makes him and you laugh; there ends the issue. This also helps a lot in a relationship, when a partner does not get angry easily and does not hold to offence more than it should be. You might slap such one and call it a joke, and there he sees it as a joke so far as you can prove beyond reasonable doubt that it is a joke. You need a partner that can take your excesses and still loves you. He might instead of getting angry with your mistakes always, make fun of them always. What may make an average person to be angry doesn't really make a person who is humorous angry; that is his nature. And the way this person settles quarrels baffles others a lot. An issue arise, a very serious issue; you expect this humorous person to organize a court proceedings to resolve such; hell no, you are very wrong. Just like a normal joke, the trouble is discussed and settled amicably.

And there comes another spark a humorous person adds in a relationship and also in the life of a partner. Very fun to be with, because he makes you happy when you are sad. When you think you have a very boring day or very bad time this one goes a long way to spice you up changing your mood almost immediately. The more you find yourself hurting, the more this person makes your heart loosen up; and relationship needs such fun to be enjoyable too. It is not just a lecture class where you keep learning about each other; it is also a playground where you both go out to play and be happy. Most people don't like to have a relationship with a person that is not fun to be with. This person that does not have that joke in him when you try to make a joke, he takes offence. You will always be afraid not to say what will hurt him. And your meeting with such person; call it a date or a soiree, becomes just a board meeting, only to discuss meeting agenda and go. Nothing like AOB and this makes your relationship boring and devoid of fun.

So this is more the reason a humorous person stands a chance to be the right person to be in a relationship with, than a person that is not. This does not really mean that every humorous person is the better person to be in a relationship with. It means that, if such one will make a better partner, like if he possesses those qualities of the right person, he tends to be a better option, than non-humorous person even when a non-humorous person possesses such good qualities too. It takes flexibility to be humorous. One who takes little things seriously all the time will not be humorous. If you are in a relationship with someone that is flexible and not too mean; you have more chances to enjoy such relationship.

I found out again that people who are humorous tend to apologize easily more than people who are not. This is because they have a soft

YES, ONLY TO THE RIGHT PERSON

nature to always not want to hurt others, and when they do in the course of living a life of joke, they quickly open up to apologize calling it a joke. And you understand it that way without feeling too hurt. You can easily forgive a humorous person than one who is not; it is simple; he is always not serious all the time. He calls you an idiot and says sorry that he was joking, and you take it that way. But one that is not humorous will call you sweetheart, and maybe you heard only "sweet" and didn't hear the "heart", you may take it as an offence, because this one is always serious with matters. How could he call you sweet, so you are now a lollipop? You might be wondering. The other time, I was watching a comedy show and one of the comedians came on the stage describing himself as stupid and mentally imbalance, and people kept laughing louder at this joke. Tell me how you will get too angry when this supposed 'stupid' person says stupid things to you. What others might find serious, this one might find it funny. This will be a very great advantage to your relationship when you have such one as a partner.

So this person, does he really show a sign of having in him humorous nature? If not, you really might be in a tight corner, always being careful dealing with such a mean person. And the more one is humorous, the more such person has a happy heart always radiating with joy that will always diffuse into the relationship; and you being a beneficiary unknowingly. A joyful heart finds it hard to spew anger and animosity even when provoked; the reason is having enough reserve of happiness to cushion the effect of that provocation. In a relationship, you will be better off if your partner is humorous. Again, it takes great intelligence to coin out words or act to make people of divergent personalities to laugh at different times. This humorous partner shows that he is such an intelligent one to do that. One with such wisdom will always understand situations to maneuver even when it seems that he is in a tight corner. The same way he could make different personalities in the audience to laugh is the same way he will understand your complexities and still make you laugh. He is likely going to make a wonderful partner.

While this quality is kept at the last part of this section is really to show that all other qualities come before it; but it still remains a quality that may likely distinguish one from others. The reason is that somehow upbringing, situations and so many internal and external factors might tend to make one not to be humorous. But then if such be the case, one that is humorous by nature always finds it easy to regain back himself due to his wonderful personality created to laugh even in time of distress. If one exhibits qualities that make him fun to be with, then there are good chances that he might not really make a wrong partner. You will always see in him a partner that takes life not too serious and not too unserious. No matter how you wrong this person in a relationship, you will always find something to make him forgive, since his humorous nature has made him to always find it easy to see life as a joke in itself.

Part Two
Negative Signs (Danger signs)

Introduction

"Love is no game. People cut their ears off over this stuff. People jump off the Eiffel Tower and sell their possessions and move to Alaska to live with the grizzly bears, and then they get eaten and nobody hears them when they scream for help. That's right. Falling in love with the wrong person is pretty much the same thing as being eaten alive by a grizzly bear." - Jess Rothenberg.

Nobody wants to get hurt in the process of loving someone; but sadly it happens. The reason being as a result of people rushing into relationship unprepared, and also ignorant of those danger signs that will likely show they will get hurt. This part deals with those danger signs that you will see in a person and know that he will likely be a wrong person, and at the end, hurt you. Though this person might exhibit very few of the good qualities already discussed; but seeing any of these negative signs will alert you, that you might be heading for doom. One that ignores this warning when visibly seen in a partner ends up with regrets after he must have made commitment in the relationship. Such person, his heart tricked him, thinking that the person will change. In this part, we will discuss seventeen signs that when this partner exhibits any, be ready to quit because he is not likely to be the right person. Do not think that it doesn't really matter, after all the person has some of those good qualities discussed. Though every human being will have a flaw, but some flaws are a threat to relationship and if you really want to be happy in your relationship, you must be ready to avoid people with such serious flaws. These signs make it clear

YES, ONLY TO THE RIGHT PERSON

also that the person does not truly love you the way you think or made to believe, you are just a prey. Even if the person loves you, you will not likely want to get eaten by grizzly bear, so to say; in the name of love.

Sign 1

Makes You Do What is Bad

"You may not know that you are doing it the way I want you to do it. You may not know you are going down the pit with me. But I know that you must do it just like I want you, because I want to destroy you like I have destroyed me because I don't really love you."
- O.D. Chimex.

How else to describe someone that makes you do wrong things, than a bad associate. How else to describe someone that makes you go against what is normal, than a bad company? Not just in friendship, in relationship too. A partner could influence the other doing what is bad, and such partner could as well be termed bad associate. You may have seen someone who finds it very difficult to tell lies, but as soon as he begins associating with someone who lies a lot, he becomes a pathological liar. It happens often and it boils down to bad influence. Not just lying, other sorts of serious bad characters too. So many times I have read the newspapers, watched the television about couple who indulged in crimes and one of the spouses often confessed that it was the other person that influenced him. Relationship, if it is with the right person will always make you a better person, know this. It is really pathetic that some are so naïve to consent to doing bad thing,

YES, ONLY TO THE RIGHT PERSON

just to please their partner. When a person you are in a relationship pressures you to do what is bad or what you are not happy doing, then the person is telling you in essence that he wants to destroy you and not to love you. If you keep doing what is bad, being sad all the time, just to please a selfish partner, how then do you think you will ever be happy in such a relationship? This sign makes it obvious that this partner pushing you to do what is bad is just a wrong person.

He is really a selfish person and does not want to know or care about how you feel; and at the same time is equally a bad company. This cut across some awful characters that you really know are repugnant, yet he pressures you to do them, just to prove that you love him. Don't be surprised that with such a person you will end up being destroyed, a totally changed bad person. Tim since married lived separately from in a small city more like a semi-urban city, because of his job. His family was living far away from him; he visited them only on weekends and returned back. This man was a very gentle man that hated trouble, he loved and saw dialogue as the only means of settling trouble, always wanted to be at peace with everybody. But then things changed when his wife and children moved in with him. After one year, Tim changed from very quiet man to a troublesome man, always pugnacious, malicious and vindictive. This sudden change in character was his wife's influence on him. Immediately his wife relocated, everybody in the neighborhood became enemy with the family. This woman was such stroppy and she was very aggressive too. As time went on, Tim's new learnt attitude caused him his job and made him enemy with everyone in the neighborhood.

Just as Tim, one could be a victim of such bad influence if his partner is the wrong one. On a more serious note, someone might go into a crime when he has a bad partner. Nobody will want to be in a relationship where he has to change for the worse; it should be the other way round. When a person is making you to change for that worse, then it simply means that the person is likely not a good partner for you.

Have you found yourself being more aggressive, greedy, selfish, and disrespectful; or even worse of it, doing what is really against the law or humanity? Then it really means you are with the wrong person and that you are being influenced badly. This is evident in some relationships, even marriages, as soon as some get married; they become enemies with their family members, friends and relatives. They become breakers of laws instead of custodians of laws. If you keep changing from good to bad maybe one day this same person will make you change to a devil incarnate. One who is the right person will always try to make you more angelic and not devilish. It is only a bad company that will change you for bad. Then if that be the case, why wasting your time with a bad company? You have seen that it has become the order of the day that such person always cajoles you into doing what is bad to please him. Don't think it was those few times, just to save the relationship; soon you will end up saving the relationship and destroying yourself. Though sometimes serious situation warrants doing something funny for a loved one, but that may likely be justified only when the life of that loved one is at stake, and no other person's life is endangered in that course.

Some do drugs not because they love doing it, but because they want to please their partners. If you partner will be so heartless to make you do what you know will destroy you, then why think that the person loves you? You really don't need a seer to tell you that that person making you to do badly hates you. Let us compare it with the love a good parent has for his children. You may have heard about families where one of the parents engages in bad habits, this person knows that what he does is bad, and he tries as much as possible to hide it from his family. The reason is because he loves them and doesn't want to destroy them the way he is destroying himself. No good mother will like her child to learn her bad ways, the same with a good father. And if one you are in a relationship with wants you to learn the bad ways, then the person will not make a good partner.

YES, ONLY TO THE RIGHT PERSON

Your relationship should be that iron that sharpens iron for good and not for bad. This is the time for you to make an honest examination of the person you are in a relationship with and see if this person has influenced you for good and not for bad. The person might not really directly make you do badly, but for the fact that the person's influence on you is in a negative direction, then the person is simply a bad company and nothing more. Your good potentials need to be harnessed and not to be exploited or dissipated. You need someone who has good motives and not bad one for you. If care is not taken, such a bad person will simply destroy you and plunge you into calamity. There is no need of paying a deaf ear and playing blind to this serious issue.

Does this person want you to be an addict like him and you think that the person is making you both to love the same thing? Hell no, the person is simply in effect telling you that you matter not to him. Do not deceive yourself by thinking that you staying in that relationship will change the person. Imagine your friend is an armed robber, and you think that you should stay with him to change him. Then a day will come when the police will either arrest both of you and charge you both for robbery, or the person's enemy will attack you in the company of the person. So in essence, your life is not safe with someone who is a bad company. A bad company is always a bad company; the only person than can change the person is the person himself, if he wants to. He can only change when he makes up his mind that he will change. Though marriage is for better for worse, but relationship is, with the better for good. Do not blindly go into commitment hoping to also take the bad, quit when it is not late to do so.

That person changing you into something bad truly doesn't love you; no criminal will like to employ rogues in his company. So if a criminal having bad behaviors will equally want a good a person, then why will you a good person want a bad person? Again this negative influence on you might not really come from the person, but the person's nasty behaviours indirectly make you to always do what you really don't like doing. Assuming, you always get drunk whenever you go out with this person. He knows that his actions expose you to doing drugs, yet he goes further to cause you to do those bad things. He is just using you as an end to his means, sooner than later you will be that his means that end you. If someone makes you to do what is bad, often or occasionally, then such a person is just the wrong one.

Sign 2

Makes Material Request From You Always

"I request materially from you always because I know that it is your wealth I want always and not you."
- O.D. Chimex.

"Please remember those items I asked you to get for me. Please I haven't received that money you promised me. Please darling, I really need this." These may be the very statements that you will always get to hear from this person most of the time. The only thing that comes to your mind any time you want to meet him is to be prepared to have a bag full of gift items, or else you won't be welcomed properly. The more you try to satisfy these requests, the more they tend to be insatiable, and soon, you might become the person's bank account. This is very obvious that the person really doesn't love you; yes the person is not for you, believe it or not. Even if he loves you, one day he will go with another who has a bigger offer than you. Don't even think that such outrageous requests are borne out of inevitable needs. Though one you are in a relationship with, might really when necessary beg you for something, but when one constantly makes material request from you, it is obvious the person is the wrong person. In my locality, I have heard some girls say that the only way to make men stop disturbing them is to make material request on them. And they mean business, even if the person has so much to spend, they don't change their mind to loving the person. The same goes with men who also boast of hoodwinking innocent ladies to surrender their material resources to them in the name of love, they simply want to dupe such naïve ones. These conmen will go a long way making all sorts of pathetic stories to whip up the person's emotions as to yielding to their requests. The wrong person's focus will be to get materially from you as much as he could, and then go his way.

This person you are in a relationship with constantly gives you one excuse or the other for you to cough out money; it then shows the person is a weasel. The funny thing is that such requests always come by sudden and often; and also this person expects you to always come with surprise gifts. The truth remains that the right person even though might have financial troubles to deal with will not be eager to tell you about it. This is because this right person doesn't want to put unnecessary burden on you because he cares about you as well. In fact most times, you will be the one to keep asking the person what the problem is, before he opens up. And that opening up is not really to force you to solve that financial problem, but to bare his mind to you. Some are really cunning; they will keep making that financial request in such a way that you will find it very difficult to understand the game being played on you. This treacherous person will cunningly whip up your emotions and make you feel being compelled to help out. He will always paint situations so badly that money requested from you seems to be needed badly than you think.

He is just proving to be the wrong person, playing a game on you and when you try to have mixed feelings about these outrageous requests, coercion becomes the weapon to use in blindfolding you. Such coercion also comes in disguise, like romance or any other enticing things. Some might come in a lottery form, giving you peanuts and

YES, ONLY TO THE RIGHT PERSON

getting huge sum in return from you. No wonder people still fall prey to internet fake lovers, some of the times. These internet weasels always keep demanding excessively from the naïve partner, cooking up stupid sympathetic stories to dupe the other person. That is the same way these wrong people operate in a relationship. If you don't agree with this, then when such a partner makes a financial request on you, say no blatantly without giving room for mixed feelings. Immediately you say no, such person will make some nasty comments or gesture and then gradually he starts to distance himself from you. You will notice that the love he showers on you will begin to dwindle, unlike when the requests were being obliged. Yes the amount of love you receive depends on the amount of money you cough out, believe it or not. Spend little, then get little love, and spend more, then be ready to be showered with more love. Any moment you get this person a gift, he becomes an angel, even if you slap him at the moment, you get a kiss back in return.

Charles my very good friend told me a story about his last relationship, how it ended in such a messy way. At first he thought he has found that perfect person to spend the rest of his life with, having seen a wonderful woman so pretty too. Not until after one year, this lady began requesting materially from him, although she wasn't doing that initially, but that change of game insinuated something. Charles though tried his best to keep up with this demand, until the lady made a very outrageous request that was almost one third of Charles monthly income. Gradually he began to refuse to oblige such requests, with excuses and silence. The more he said no, the more the lady stayed far from him, until lastly what Charles heard was the lady's sudden marriage to another man. It was so devastating to him, but then it was not his fault; he took it as his fate. Few months later, the lady called Charles to tell him that actually she put up those requests to tell him indirectly that she didn't love him after all. This bad sign can come at any moment, but mostly when it comes at the start of a relationship, then you have to be at alert knowing that you are in with a business tycoon ready to make you his business.

The right person will not always be eager to demand materially from you, even though you might be the next Bill Gate. The person might not be that well to do materially, but your material worth does not matter to him; he wants something more from you than money. And also wants to be selfless rather than selfish. The person in essence is telling you that 'take your money off, he still loves you.' One making material request on you always, is telling you indirectly that without your money that there will be nothing like the relationship. You see the person lacking materially, yet the person seldom asking for your material possessions, that is to say he has the relationship at heart. In fact, it is only lazy people that keep depending on other people for material support. One who is wise enough and hardworking will want to be independent, and that is the kind of person you really need. No wonder some that ignored this warning signs and went into marriage found out that no matter their partner's abundant wealth, the person still asks for more. You see some spouse will have lots of money in their account, yet they want their mates to spend that last money in his account, they don't care if that mate will go bankrupt thereafter. This is the highest point of selfishness and, 'I don't really care' attitude. It didn't start newly, just that one person fell to recognize those time the other person was making those outrageous material requests, or maybe, neglected. And this neglected sign goes on and into the marriage becoming a bone of contention.

The right person will always want to give you like it has been discoursed earlier, and not to take from you. This shows that it is a typical real relationship with the right person, coming to give and not to take. That you are having abundant will not deter the person from giving you; and that you have so much will as well not make the person to demand from you. Any gift does not change the way such a person's treats you, though sometimes gift tend to alter the way some act toward

YES, ONLY TO THE RIGHT PERSON

the benefactor. Gift or no gift, the relationship will not be altered and treatment will be the same. Again, the right person will still take your heaven and earth and will still look into your face and tell you lovingly that you are wrong when you are wrong. But the wrong person will take those gifts, telling you are right when you are wrong, even when such spiel will cause you something serious. The reason is simple, your gifts matter a lot more than you, and so they should not be missed.

Do not be misled, such wrong people will always move fast toward you trying to bewitch you and you think such melodramatic moves are for real. The more you try to understand what really is happening, the more you see yourself going deeper into the mess. Even if you have more than enough to throw about, you may give out to such one, but have it in mind that such person will not likely make a good partner. The reason is simply; your wealth is what he is after. And you think you are equal to the task to buy this person at all cost; then be ready to have this person surprise you when you don't expect it. This surprise always comes with making you know that he has no feelings for you.

Sign 3

Takes Offense at Every Little Thing

*"Do you know why I constantly let you know that every little thing you do irritates me? I do it because I really don't want you around me anymore." - **O.D. Chimex.***

You can only become irritated with someone that you don't want around you. No matter what good this person does, you find it hard to appreciate such a person. It happens not just between casual friends, it could happen in a relationship too, and it implies only but one thing, that you are not wanted. Every little thing becomes an issue to make you feel bad, this only the wrong person uses as a weapon to distance himself from you. And you are still blind to notice that this person is the wrong person; he doesn't love you for real and you keep forcing the relationship to work. Though he might make a good partner, but definitely not for you, but for another person he wants. This clear fact I wonder why some people still find it hard to understand and they keep pushing harder to be wanted by a person that rejects them. If you still insist, get ready to receive a shocker sooner than later. In a right relationship, it has been proven that love covers mistakes, no matter how often. Yes this is absolutely correct, that is why when you are with the wrong person who doesn't love you, the person takes offence at every little thing you do. He is in essence telling you that you

YES, ONLY TO THE RIGHT PERSON

are not needed and loved. Everything you do irritates him and you think he is not the wrong person? It will come to the point that you even get afraid to do anything with this person; the reason is because everything you do, he finds fault in it. You have noticed this, yet you still want to be in that relationship and I will ask you: for what reason? My dear you should start to see this person as the wrong person and this display is just to make you find your way. You can only take a horse to the stream, but cannot force it to drink the water. Those things the person makes you think you always do wrongly are really not done wrongly. It is just that he has refused to accept you the way you are, to tell you that your presence irritates him.

Tell me one good reason a right person will make you feel that you are always wrong and doesn't do what is right. Even if you do it rightly sometimes, but for the fact that you are with a person that hates you, you will feel that you do it wrongly. You don't need a relationship where you have to be at alert like a hummingbird, simply because you don't want to offend your partner. Never will you have peace of mind if you are with such one. Even someone who is very careless and bad might at sometimes do it rightly. There is this story I read in a book, about a particular man. It happened that this man was so bad that he was seen as a devil by the whole community. Then he died and a priest must officiate at his burial as their tradition demanded. The priest knew all about this bad man, but he had to be buried, since he was an active member of his church. Just at the burial ground, this priest who has never heard anything good about this dead bad man and has never seen him do good; was in a catch-22 as to what good to say about this evil man. He looked at the man in the coffin and looked at the few relatives and sympathizers at the burial ground and said: "I have never seen a person with such a wonderful set of white teeth like this man." And yes he was correct, every person even though bad, must have something good. You don't really need to worry yourself much thinking maybe that the reason behind the action of finding fault in all you do is because you do it wrongly all the time. The reason is that he doesn't want you, right in his heart.

The person you are dating or should date should as well also see your wonderful set of white teeth, even though you might be bad. But for the fact that he takes offense at every little thing you do means that he is the wrong person for you. Even if you continue to try your possible best to please him, to him you will always do it wrongly, just a way to get rid of you is what he is thinking about. He will ask you to do it this way and immediately you do it that way, he will in turn find a fault in that thing. You will continue trying your best to please this person till you totally lose yourself, becoming a moron. And the worse is that at last the person will still turn around to kick you out because you are just unwisely tenacious. Since you have continued to fail his test of not seeing the handwriting on the wall, one day, he will write not on the wall again but in your face.

If this person you is showing you that everything you do is done wrongly, then tell the person that the relationship is as well the wrong one and that the person is really the wrong person for you. The most subtle way of finding fault in whatever you do is by character; some are bold enough and insolent to tell in words that you are always at fault; some by actions. He might be telling you by actions that you are faulty all the time, and if you are not smart enough, you might find it difficult to understand. That grimace, that hissing, and sighing, what else do you need to be told that they show he doesn't accept what you have done? Another common way such a person does that is by being an ingrate. Does not show appreciation to what you do, always sighing at every little thing you do. Everything you do, you see his mood immediately changes, this will tell you that he abhors you. You have done your best and expect to be at least appreciated, you are just wrong, just that forceful thank you, if not a 'no thank you.' You might have smartly, some of the times, noticed this nasty mood change and you tried to ask what the problem was, the next thing the person did was to smartly say:

YES, ONLY TO THE RIGHT PERSON

"Nothing." And you naively believed that there was nothing; and he quickly puts up a fake smile, making you believe all is well. This is because it might not really be up to the time he lets you go; he might be gaining something from you at the moment. Wait until he is done with you, and you must go. Right in the person's heart he says: "This fool, I wish you could just let me be." And you might push and keep pushing to please him, the next attitude he comes up with is keeping silent on everything you do, even if it is so glaring that you are not doing it well and need to be lovingly corrected, this person will just be agreeing to whatever stupid things you do. Because you really don't matter to him, and it stays that way, that is more the reason he takes offence at every little thing that you do.

The more you work harder to improve and expect him to show appreciation at your earnest effort, the more wrong you are. He will not appreciate what effort you have put, even if it will cost you a fortune of either your time or your finance. If a person professes love for you and still thinks that you are just a rotten fruit without any benefit, then what kind of love is that? You keep apologizing even when it is obvious that the fault is his; hell no, you must receive the whole lambasting first before he stops. You keep making this person see reason for you being remorseful yet you have to be crucified first. And you still don't think he is the wrong person? This exact person that makes you pay for every wrong you do either by neglecting you or by beating you with words tells you that you really are with the wrong person. In a relationship with the right person, you have worth and your worth should always be acknowledged, those little things you err will not warrant offence to be taken. You don't need someone to keep making you sad, implying that you are a failure all the time, it does distract you. Only the wrong the person will do this to you. You need someone who will at all times make you have peace so as to achieve something meaningful. This, the right person knows and will continue to help you, making you a better person, even if you always err.

Sign 4

Slow About Initiating Conversation

"Just like my heart has grown cold with you, the same way my words have grown cold. If you like force the words out of my mouth; the only thing I know is that I can't force the words out first, because I want you out first."

- O.D. Chimex.

The mention of this heading will leave some with mixed feelings, wondering if actually this really counts in getting to know if a person is for real. But the fact remains that conversation really does a lot of work in a relationship, exposing ones intention and not just thoughts and feelings. Some may go on to say that after all, some are born introverts, they are not really always eager to spark off conversation unless they are made to. You may be a bit right if you go on to defend the fact that some are slow in speaking. But when it comes to relationship, this is another sign that will make you come to terms that this person is not really into you. The more someone wants you, the more the person will be eager to initiate a conversation with you. Some have failed to understand that initiating a conversation does not only involve talking; it as well involves gestures and body movements. These unseen aspects of the person will convince you that this person

YES, ONLY TO THE RIGHT PERSON

wants your company always. Even animals, when two opposite sex are together enjoying the company of one another, they tend to make funny sounds. And if they are not making sounds, they use body gestures to show that they enjoy each other's company. If one finds it hard to initiate conversation with you, you are the one always doing it all the time, then know it that you are not in the person's heart.

It is only one who doesn't like you will be slow to initiate a conversation with you. The person sees conversing with you as a waste of time and vain thing. Why should he start up a conversation with you when really he is not interested in having a conversation with you? You are just a bore to the person and this you have failed to realize. Each time you try to strike up a conversation with him, he will be looking for an excuse to cut the conversation as soon as possible; you don't really impress him. Take for instance if you are chatting on a social network with this particular friend, you find out that each time, you are the one to force the person to chat with you. Does that not really show you that he is not interested in chatting with you? The person is telling you that there are lots of things that need his attention more than you, so you better not bug him with your boring conversation. If one is such a person that always tells you that you are such a bore, how then do you think that such one is for real? What other sign do you need to be shown that you are really chasing after the wind?

Assuming at the onset, this person you want to start a relationship with displays this attitude toward you, you may for the benefit of the doubt take it as just shyness or as a result of being new to each other. But if this continues or becomes a reoccurring thing, then it has gone beyond benefit of the doubt, it is a clear sign that you are not wanted. You are not doing yourself any favour if you keep pushing this person to converse with you. It is only like poles that will attract like poles, if your conversation doesn't move this person; then you are not attracted to him. Some don't see this as a clear sign that they are with the wrong person, who might likely not be interested in them. Don't be naïve; if one doesn't feel like saying hi to you, then you are not in the person's memory. Even in an already started relationship, when the line of communication continues to dwindle, know that it is a sign that the relationship is about hitting the rock. It shows that something is wrong somewhere.

Conversation is one of the most important ingredients that helps the relationship to flow; it does the same work a lubricant does to the engine, to the relationship. Your car might be in good order, have enough fuel in the tank, but if it lacks oil, soon the car will be doomed. The reason is simple, if you don't often discuss about things that will strengthen the relationship, then how will the relationship thrive? If you don't have a good line of communication, how will you develop a bond? The same way if that person finds it difficult to initiate a conversation and you are the only person who seems to enjoy the other person's company, then how will the relationship thrive? Unless you want to run a one man show, then be ready to pay the heavy price.

You are the one who makes the call, the one who texts and the one that always ask for both to have a time out together. Then it means you are the only one that thinks that the relationship needs to go on. You are the only person who dwells in the illusion that a relationship exist between both. The other person is as good as dormant waiting for you to make the first move and if you don't, so will it be. But it seems that you are deeply in love and you don't even count it as something; my dear, it matters a lot. Like it was said earlier, relationship is a two way thing, 50:50, if it must work well, the two people must make it to work. No amount of busy schedule will make the person to give as an excuse for not always starting a conversation or initiating that move to have a conversation with you.

Sometimes you hear couple shouting at each other: "You saw my texts and my calls and: why didn't you text or call back?" Why would the person text you back when it is obvious that you are just a bore?

YES, ONLY TO THE RIGHT PERSON

Why should the person call you back when it is obvious that there are more important things than you? I mean this person is in essence making you see that you really don't worth his time. Some will be so smart to always shout in surprise and give lots of excuses, pacifying the offended that they really forgot. But then the same person keeps forgetting all the time. That is just the trick, he uses that to make you not to feel sad, and you believe the crap? Search the person's memory, heart, even his mind, you are not there at all, and that is why he doesn't like starting up a conversation, because you are practically nonexistent in his mind. Even if he is by birth an introvert or slow in speaking, then let the person always be the one to make you feel that you really are wanted. Saying just hi is enough to tell you that the person wants to have your time. Smiling at you when you both talk, shows that your company interests him. But that cold and aloof attitude, show that really, time with you is not worth it.

I was with a friend a particular day, he opened up to me that a lady he was trying to start up a relationship with finds it difficult to take his calls, and even if she takes the call, she gives excuses on why she wouldn't be able to talk to him at that moment till further time. Sometimes she will cut the call and tell him she will call back, and that ends it till the man himself calls back. This friend was really asking me what these attitudes meant. I felt pity for him, because he was so naïve to see the writing on the wall. "Hey, my man, you are really with the wrong person, so don't waste your time chasing after the wind." That was my honest reply to him. He thought such actions are expected when a relationship is at the early stage; he didn't believe me. As that same attitude continued, he took it upon himself to interrogate the girl why she seldom calling him or picking his calls. And to his utmost surprise the lady spilled the beans that she really didn't want to start a relationship with him. That he was just forcing her into starting a relationship she was not ready for. The same is with such one that finds it hard to start or have a conversation with you; you might be the only one that wants the relationship.

Like earlier said, that seldom or reluctance in starting a conversation with you is a very obvious sign that that person does not want that relationship. In his mind, no relationship exist, but to you, you think it exists. You have not been told it doesn't exist, simply because you are pressuring him at the moment. To avoid a shock, you are made to assume that something exists. And the most subtle way to tell you off is to widen the gap between you and him. He is making you believe that you are wanted, whereas you are not. And as soon as the person gets what he wants or feel it is right time to let you know, if you keep pressuring him, he tells you.

Sign 5

Argument Becomes the Order of the Day

"We argue a lot and shout at each other even when we are close to each other. The reason is that our hearts are fifty miles away from each other; sorry we are not compatible." - O.D Chimex.

The moment you think that an argument has just ended, another more serious one will erupt. Several times you have tried to talk things out, but it seems it is not working. Every little thing ends in argument means not only that you both are not compatible; it also means that so many things are against you. It maybe character-wise, hobby-wise, taste-wise, choice-wise and many other things that show that you both are not meant to be together. This is exactly the sad truth about wrong relationship, and it is also as good as saying that you both are wrong partners for each other. You might not really point out which of you is wrong. The partners might really be working so hard to make it work, but the unseen forces are also working so hard as well to make it not to work. There are whole lots of things that seem not to be working in such relationship, showing that the coming together to form an alliance will fail. You do not need a seer to tell you that the compatible is not there. This might become so bad that you both find discussion and being together more of a war. Character-wise, the two might not be bad, but so many things come in-between to prove that you are not meant to be together. It is a sign to show that the relationship will not work no matter how hard you try; instead one person will end up being hurt.

Humans are so unique and sophisticated more than any living thing in the world. Despite this divergence it is funny also to know that there are always combinations of two people that will easily be achievable, leading to a wonderful cohabitation. Two people might be very good if they are paired to other people in relationships, but bring those same two people and pair them together, they will not find it funny to make a good relationship. And this form the basis of people knowing their weaknesses and strengths before going into a relationship so as to get just the opposite who will be a perfect match. Ignorance in understanding this will make one person assume that the other person is the wrong person. You might think that it is in the other person's nature to argue on every little thing; that might be far from the truth. No way will you both make good partners, and that is the reason for those constant arguments, telling you to not waste your time trying to make a relationship that will never work.

Tell me how a relationship will work, if you both keep on arguing on everything, without coming to agreement? Even if you just settle an argument now, any little thing will spark up another. Maybe one of you has made enquiries about the other person to see if such person always has issues with others. To his surprise, the person finds it hard to argue with others, yet the relationship is replete with constants arguments. And the more arguments become the order of the day, the more your hearts get farer from each other, the two hearts can never come together. This becomes like an experiment we made when we were kids. Then, we will get two magnets of repelling sides and forced them together. We went as far as clenching and tying them together thinking that after sometimes they will get used to each other and come to magnet. Days, weeks and months, passed, as soon as the two was

YES, ONLY TO THE RIGHT PERSON

untied, they quickly repelled each other. This will always be the case when two incompatible people come together in a relationship, no matter how good they are, they have very slim chances of making the relationship work. And this, the constant arguments are telling you.

No matter how you both try to avoid argument it surely must always be the order of the day. And in some cases, these unbridled arguments end up in fights. Ask yourself if you will like a relationship where even two angels will always be fighting? In this case no one is to be blamed for the arguments, just that you both are not compatible. Some may not be wise enough to understand, they might be thinking that it is the other person that is always to be blamed. And the other person too, shifting the blame to the other one as well. The relationship simple means the wrong one, so to say. Relationship filled with lots of arguments is a very bad one, especially when the parties have tried a lot to stop it, yet it continues. The arguments simple shows that they have a conflicting views as a result of conflicting personalities. Then how could a relationship work, when two people involved have divergent personalities and they are handicapped to harmonize it into a synergy? The simple term for it is that you are just two enemies deceiving yourselves thinking you are friends in a relationship. Take for instance two pilots in the same cockpit, each with different map, yet they profess that they are flying to the same destination. They will keep dragging which of the maps to follow till the aircraft crashes. In a good relationship, the parties must have that compatibility even though they are different. If they don't, no need being in that relationship, they will only be wasting their time.

Lots of arguments in a relationship prove that nobody wants to support each other, and a relationship that nobody supports each other is always bound to fail sooner than later. Both of you must not always have the same view or agree all the time; but the team work and the compatibility is that those different views should always be harmonized so as to achieve a single purpose which will in turn benefit both maximally. But since both of you find it difficult to harmonize your views or when unseen forces always make it stupid to harmonize the views; then it means that you are in the wrong relationship. For these reasons you have to be at alert to observe if your relationship is replete with arguments, and if that be the case, sorry you are both wrong to be in a right relationship.

Do not take this for granted, argument is a very serious issue in a relationship especially when it becomes a norm. In fact it sparks all other troubles and makes it easy for the parties to have an excuse to do things that will hurt the relationship. Some people who are unfaithful will always cite argument as one of the reasons for their act; same with people who beat their spouse. So why work so hard to make that car move when there are no tires on it? This issue is very germane to take it into consideration in any relationship. If you give it time and yet, the constant arguments persist, don't be blind to take the bull by the horn. Though a trouble might come up to make a relationship to be in jeopardy with constants barrage of arguments. But in the absence of this trouble, just that both of you find it hard to agree on things almost all the time, is a clear sign that no head way will be made in such relationship. You might try to ignore this warning sign, agreeing to make it work by force, but that is more disastrous. People that ignore this end up in a marriage they will still end soon. Each person goes on trying as much as possible to accommodate the other, yet both will be hurting in the process. A day will come when you both will find it very difficult to hold the two negative sides of magnet together. This day might be after a serious commitment must have been made, that is marriage, or emotions are seriously involved. For instance, how do you expect two people that talk too much to always relate well, since each one will be after speaking his mind? Nobody is ready to be a good listener. It will only take a talkative and a good listener to cohabit well, since one is good at talking and the other is good at listening. These

YES, ONLY TO THE RIGHT PERSON

constant arguments after all efforts have been made, are telling you both to look for the right partners.

Relationship with the right persons will always be a place where two people with different ideologies, views, opinions, will see a connection that will harmonize this diversity as a result of their make-up, upbringing, and educational background, social and religious status, to achieve a single goal, which is a perfect relationship. Anything short of this, is a bad relationship.

Sign 6

Derogatory Words Without Feeling Remorse

"When dealing with people, remember you are not dealing with creatures of logic, but creatures of emotion."
- Dale Carnegie.

Words are abstract but they always cut even deeper than a two-edge sword. It is sad most people in the world today are not mindful of this fact; and as a result they talk before thinking. This always hurt others especially when the person is someone very close. When this becomes a norm, then it depicts danger. Like every other danger signs in a bad relationship, often use of derogatory words by a partner is another quick sign that will make you to come to term that you are with someone that will likely make a bad partner. It also connotes that the person likely does not have deep regard for you in his heart. This sharp cutting with words tends to cause a wound so bad that will never likely heal in a short time. If this partner makes unpleasant remarks about you at every opportunity, this is evidence that you are in a bad relationship; so start making a U-turn. Words said are not taking back; it goes forth till it reaches the final consumer. Words can heal as well as kill, and the killing is the worst type of killing, because it kills

YES, ONLY TO THE RIGHT PERSON

gradually damaging the most precious part of you. These are what derogatory words do to the receiver. Why then will you like to be in a relationship with someone that is always killing you with words? We say words we always regret sometimes, especially to those we don't really love, value and respect. Those we love from the heart, we are very cautious to say words that will hurt them, and when such words are said out of the workings of imperfection, we feel remorseful and want to take those words back, although it might be too late. If that be the case, then it means that when we keep saying such nasty words to those we claim to love, it means we actually don't love such ones.

Relationship should be a haven where encouraging words are spew out all the time to build each other so as to be happy, that is the essence of love. Even if there is a cause to make a harsh remark, caution is always applied to avoid hurting others. If a relationship is bereft of this, then the evidence is clear that really it is a bad relationship with the wrong person. Some find themselves in relationship where derogatory words become the order of the day and they are yet to come to terms that the relationship is a bad one. For Christ's sake what again do you need to understand that this person that always cuts you with words hates you? Even if he professes that he loves you, don't you think those words will keep breaking you whenever they are said? You need to be built up and not to be put down; and that is the reason you go into a relationship to be augmented by the other person. You get into a slight misunderstanding with this person you are in a relationship with and the next thing is to be called names like you were some sort of garbage. Instead of addressing you with words that make you feel priceless, you are addressed with words that make you feel worthless simple because of just a minor mistake. When you need mild and loving correction from your partner, you get a nasty bashing. When you need encouragement to do it better another time, you get a tongue-lashing for doing it wrongly. This person is really a bad person, maybe you are yet to understand. He is telling you that you worth nothing and if you still want to make a head way with such relationship, you are in essence accepting to worth nothing.

Most times you see lots of people being in abusive relationships, they say a whole lot of things about how their partner used to talk badly at them, and these people still stay in the relationship. Although I might not really put the blame on them because their emotions have caged them, they seem to not want to see this as a sign of being in a relationship with the wrong person. To them, they have been blindfolded by love, and seem to take this for granted. No matter how the love comes, and no matter how this person puts a façade, the truth is that one that uses derogatory words on you all the time seem to either have fallen out of love with you or been the wrong person to hand over your heart to. If you take your time to ask people who have broken up with a partner, they will always tell you that at some time, that partner became so abusive with derogatory words almost all the time.

Admittedly, once in a while one might lose his temper on the one he loves, but when such happens, the right person does not go on to show that loss of temper with bad words. He might show that loss of temper with raising of voice, but not with raising of sarcastic words that will cut you like an axe. These words continue to cut you even after they have been said, and this person cares not to know about the effects of the words. And in a situation where spontaneously a right person used derogatory words on you, outright show of remorse will follow immediately to assuage and atone for the nasty words. This is not the first, neither the second, such person used such words, it has become a constant occurrence, and you still think it is a mistake. If the bad words are said mistakenly out of anger, then the right person will try as much as possible to make reparation by not saying such again, at least not in the nearest future. But the wrong person, will not care about the words, in fact be ready to receive more of the missiles always. He keeps saying it often and keeps apologizing often, as well.

YES, ONLY TO THE RIGHT PERSON

Love seems to be like a chain, holding down lots of people from doing badly to their loved ones. Love is a very strong emotion that could even disarm a knife-wielding villain. So assuming one due to upbringing tries to give excuses as to his reason for using derogatory words all the time, then sit down and think how many times the person has really called himself an idiot for making a mistake. This shows you that words could be restrained. Love makes one to restrain hurting other person, and hate makes one to perennially hurt others without feeling any remorse. Let us say for instance that this person was once a darling, seldom using such words on you at the onset of the relationship. But now, everything has changed, you have become a jackass to the person, and this he lets you know by those words he says.

For the fact those words are said always also means that the person lacks respect for you. How do you think you can cope in a relationship with one that doesn't have respect for you? Be at alert to recognize this as some of those negative signs that show that the relationship has gone wrong, or that you are with the wrong person. Abusive words are said out of hatred and grudge, there has been a grudge against you and the person uses every little opportunity to show you that by words. Some always defend themselves with such things like: "It is actually a slip of tongue; it is not the way it is in my heart." That is another big lie; words are exactly our heart at the moment. A person's words are just telling you: "Listen, this is how my heart is at the moment." You can't call a person a criminal if you don't think the person is a criminal. What one says is what his heart has convinced him of. And for this reason, you should know that the wrong person always uses derogatory words as means to show you how you are in his heart. His words are just a vivid picture of you in his heart and not just mere words.

What if a situation has made someone to always lose his anger at every moment with unkind words following? If a person could as well let a situation to affect him so badly that he transfers the anger on you, then he sees you as no helper. And that goes against the reason for a relationship, which is to see the other person as someone to run to in the time of trouble; someone to shelter you when others have pushed you away. Only a person likely to make the right one will understand this and not let the trouble push him into using harsh words on you.

Sign 7

Intense Jealousy

"When we get too jealous about somebody, we tell the person indirectly that: look, we don't trust you."
- O.D. Chimex.

It is quite complicating to know that jealously protects at the same time destroys a relationship; and everybody has it. How come about this complexity? You might ask. Jealousy in a relationship is like that salt that your food needs in order to taste good. Could only be a disaster when either below or above the right amount. This jealousy always comes when one wants to be the first person or the only one standing, and when that is not the case the person gets jealous. Managing this jealous in relationship in order to keep it at a balance, has remained a problem and when it tends to go above balance it serves as a danger sign. And this going above balance portrays how bad a relationship could be. Everything should always be held at a balance, Economists refer to it as finding an equilibrium point. This form the basis of some going with this notion that: "Too much of everything is bad." And that is very correct; even when you are being nice to people, too much of it will get you into trouble as well. Relationship needs a bit of jealousy that is a right amount, to prove its authenticity, like that food you put the right quantity of salt in to achieve a delicious taste.

You get to make the food a bad one if the wrong amount of salt is applied, no matter how garnished the food is. You love eating sugary things, but eat them more than required; you will be handed over a diabetes certificate sooner or later.

Intense jealousy in a relationship is another sign of a bad one; and the partner being intensely jealous, is likely going to make a wrong partner. Some naïve ones brag about how over jealous their partners are, and they think it is a sign of how much love the person has for them. Intense jealous is in essence showing how much endangered your life is in a relationship. Do you know that someone who is so jealous in a relationship can shoot you at the sight of you with your brother, if the person doesn't know your brother? She can as well rain insults on you mom if she doesn't know she is your mother, especially if your mom looks prettily slinky. This person tries to cut you off from people simply because he is so jealous about you. Think of how many times you will be interrogated like a criminal, and embarrassed in the public, just because someone of the opposite sex is having a conversation with you. I have read lots of relationship problems and I came to understand that some abusive relationship is as a result of intense jealousy on the side of one partner. And as mentioned earlier, this relationship might be embellished with other beautiful qualities, but just this intense jealous makes that relationship a bad one. I have this memorable experience that each time I remember it, I guffaw. A day I was in a shopping mall, I heard a couple arguing. The lady was with an aged man and the young man approached them and dragged her aside from the man, and the next thing I heard was: "Becky who is that old idiot?" "John, are you sure you are alright? You are addressing my father as an idiot?" The old man was just bewildered by that audacious display of insolence, as he drags her away from her father. I wonder what would have been the old man's reaction if he heard his probable son-in-law referring to him as an idiot; maybe he would never give his consent to their union. Just as a black cloth, intense jealous blinds the person making him to be so suspicious

YES, ONLY TO THE RIGHT PERSON

all the time. Every move the other partner makes becomes trouble, making that one always frustrated. The way I saw that young man, he would have slapped the lady if he was an aggressive type. And from the way things went between the two, the lady was fed up with such relationship and may soon call it quit. I was sure she would have been so unhappy in the relationship being stalked all the time.

You need to have peace of mind and you need to always not be interrogated, who you are with and where you went to. You need to be trusted and not be suspected, you need to be safe with your partner and not unsafe; but all these intense jealous from a wrong person will deny you. Imagine when this wrong person makes you feel restricted even though you are free. Your cell phone has to be checked, texts and calls, all must be reviewed at every now and then. Some will go a long way in demanding for your password so as to have access to your social network accounts. What again do you need to be told before you will come to reality that he is really a wrong person? The sad side of it is that, you get monitored while this same person walks freely without being monitored. You are the one to continue to suffer in the relationship. Tell me what difference you have with someone that is kidnapped? If you are with the right person, you will feel trusted and not suspected. You will see yourself having a peace of mind to achieve a lot and not restricted.

This wrong person with this intense jealous goes a long way to stalk you and you won't know. The more the relationship continues, the more he has chains of spies to watch you and report to him at every moment. Simply put, you are on a watch list. He goes a long way to make you look like a piece of property owned, undermining your free will. He tells his friend to monitor you and all your activities as well as your own friends are hired to watch you. And you keep being answerable to the person all the time. Should the right person subject you to these kinds of caged wall, just to prove that he wants you? No is the answer. Imagine what will become of you if the relationship develops into commitment, then you will be handed over a curfew.

People that are so jealous are not only cowards; they are also insecure people who really don't feel safe with themselves. And you think you can be secure with one who doesn't feel secure with his self? If one is such a coward always sensing danger in what seems to be not dangerous, how would such person succeed in a world full of risks? These are some of the reason you need to consider in order to convince you to distance yourself from such one that is intensely jealous in a relationship. It is not real love like some have thought, that makes one to be intensely jealous; it is just fake love with which will come to play out in future. It is a kind of love that could be likened to bag of goodies thrown into a pool with deadly crocodiles. Imagine the wonderful things that are in the bag, if you dare jump into the pool to have the bag be ready to still jump out with severe wounds. Danger sign it is in a relationship; you will soon witness with your own eyes that this person will always be wrong with his wrong assumptions of things. Big time jealous person is always living in an anachronistic dream world all the time, he tends to see an elephant where there is just an ant. Such person ends up being paranoid schizophrenic, a condition very near to mental illness. He tries to make a mountain out of a mole and tries to create trouble where there is none. And you will always be at the receiving part of it, always being a victim. If that should be the case, why would you want to be in a relationship with a person that is slightly near insanity? Tell me why you should still feel safe with someone that might at any time go haywire due to delusion? There might be love, but such love is called dangerous love.

This person is clearly proving to be wrong person for you. You will always be unhappy because he will not stop coming up with things to spoil your mood all the time. Your life also will be in danger if you keep being in a relationship with such one; unless you have a life assurance package that is sufficient enough because it is obvious that you will not

YES, ONLY TO THE RIGHT PERSON

survive in that relationship. Jealousy should always be at a balance in a relationship and when this goes out of hand it frustrates you. Though there could still be hope if a partner with intense jealousy is very willing to make a total turnaround, very visible one. This turnaround could only be acceptable when it is consistently maintained over a longer period of time. But what if after your sincere effort to make this jealous person change, it seems it is not working, know it that it is just the person's temperament, and it could endanger you if the relationship continues.

Sign 8

Constant Criticism of Your Efforts

"We can improve our relationships with others by leaps and bounds if we become encouragers instead of critics." - **Joyce Meyer.**

Efforts no matter how little should always be cherished and commended by someone who professes love for you; anything short of this might likely come from a stranger. Constant criticisms of someone's efforts go a long way to destroy instead of build the person. The moment someone criticizes your effort no matter how constructive it is; you will feel humiliated and embarrassed. It comes like a scorpion sting to the receiver. Imagine when this becomes a continuous occurrence from a partner, how debilitating it would be. More of the reason criticism should be avoided in a relationship; rather build up with correction. Support and encouragement go with love, but criticism goes with hate. One can only criticize you when he has no deep love and respect for you. When earnest effort is put, no matter how stupid it might look, one who really loves you will always build you up and support you with words of encouragement and not with criticism. Yes, some will tell you that there is constructive criticism; criticism I know, no matter how constructive it might look, hurts. I don't think one who loves you will always criticize you, rather he will lovingly advice,

YES, ONLY TO THE RIGHT PERSON

corrects and supports you. Criticism hurts so badly, and one who really have your feelings at heart will always avoid criticizing you rather should always make you feel that you really have put a good effort in that plan. When a partner constantly rubbishes your efforts, it is likely that such a person has no regard for you.

If you are in a relationship, or about to, this is another danger sign that this person doesn't really love you, the person is likely the wrong one to be in a relationship with. Imagine when you have put a wonderful time-consuming and painstakingly stressful effort, and the next thing you get from someone who professes love for you is a barrage of criticisms. This is really heartbreaking; it shatters you and slows you from making such efforts next time. If it continues, you will seldom making efforts. This is why you don't need this kind of person to be around you as your partner. You need a supporter that will make you do more and achieve more. And this support will only come from that right person. A relationship is meant to build and not to tear, to encourage and not to discourage, and if a person constantly discourages you with words such a person will not make you grow, but slow you down.

Let us look at it this way going by the dictionary definition of criticism, "disapprovingly indicate a fault." This person only indicates fault and does not acknowledge an effort, he disapproves of you and not just your efforts. Your plans may have an atom of wrongness in them, but only the wrong person will see just that wrong part and not commend that right part. You have a partner to make you achieve better plans and to support you, and that is the essence of being in a relationship. Looking at it this way, the person simply tells you that your plans are as good as stupid; therefore, stop bringing out plans since they will end up being stupid. It weighs you down and not builds you up. I personally hate criticism and love correction. Tell me areas that I need to improve and not make it look like I did a whole lot of mess, and I will always want you to be my adviser. I used to have a boss who will always criticize my effort no matter how good the effort was. He waited for my effort to tell me how wrong it was; and he found it hard to commend me so as to give room for improvement. This became part of him that I felt so afraid to use my initiative, I was afraid to put effort. I relied on him hundred percent so that when it fails, he will take the blame and not me.

This is another effect of criticism on the person being criticized constantly, gradually having a corrosive effect on you without you noticing it. You feel like your efforts are worthless, and as time goes on if the criticism continues to come, you will be very afraid to do something on your own. You will totally be relegated to a place of robot, depending solely on the other person for decisions. Will that be the kind of person you will like to spend your life with, someone that will always make you dormant? Someone that will always put you down most of the time? This person is making you solely dependent so as to exploit you the more. He puts you down because he wants to cage you and have all your activities dictated. One who loves you always sees good in you and the same goes with whatever good plan you make. The right person tells you how successful you will be when you try that new thing, and that goes a long way to motivate you to do more.

This person that constantly criticizes your efforts is likely not that right person that will help you to achieve your dream, so you better stop wasting your time with such person. If someone will not support you to achieve your own goal, he is more or less telling you to stop making efforts. In some parts of the world, some men discourage women in making plans and putting effort, for a purpose. Their aim of doing that is very simple, they want to make their women totally dependent so that they will always use that incapacitated state as a hold on, to exploit them. But should that be so with one who would make a right partner? No is the answer. A right person recognizes that your happiness depends on you not being dependent but on you carving out a niche for yourself to show your sense of belonging. Your happiness

YES, ONLY TO THE RIGHT PERSON

comes from your efforts that work. He sees you as someone with wonderful potentials that need to be harnessed and encouraged; and essential to not just your wellbeing but to the wellbeing of the relationship as well. A wrong person knows this, but simply does not really meant well for you, so he is in essence jealous of you, and wants to relegate you to the background.

Stay alert as to know when your partner or this potential partner constantly criticizes your plans, making it look as if you are good for nothing. It is a danger sign that this person will not make a good partner. He is not supportive, rather; he is destructive by words. That bad attitude of just seeing bad in what others do is very dangerous in a relationship. It weakens you, cages you, puts fear in you and finally turns you into a moron. Always being afraid and shy to try new things. Do you think then that you will thrive in this kind of relationship? Hell no, you are bound to fail either by actions or by thinking. Take for instance; the impact criticism has on a child when such comes from one of the parents. This child makes effort, but her dad or mom always tells him that he is as stupid as his efforts. A child from such home always does poorly in life; he is scared to make efforts to avoid being criticized. In the long run it goes a long way to affect the child's growth both mentally and otherwise. A wrong person will end up making you be like this child, always feeling sad and afraid thereby retarding your growth. He shows you that he is perfect while you are imperfect; and will always be an ingrate. No matter how hard you try to, you will never be appreciated. And finally will put fear in you making you not to keep trying in life, even if you are not doing it rightly.

I read this wonderful story of a man that has a bad cook as a wife. It happens that his mother visited, and as well his wife prepared a bad meal. This man was the first to taste it, and again this meal was salty as usual. Immediately he took some pinch of salt sprayed it on the meal. On tasting the food, his mother put the blame on him for the salty meal and not his wife. Out of love, he wanted to cover up for his wife's weakness, and will not stand the sight of his mother criticizing his wife. This is exactly how the right person works. You may have bad plans; you may have bunch of craps as plans, but instead of throwing them out telling you how stupid they are; they will be accommodated and then tactically modified to make sense. When criticism of your efforts becomes the order of the day, then you are in with someone that will likely make a bad partner.

Sign 9

Being Aggressive

"Three things in human life are very important: the first is to be kind; the second to be kind; and the third is to be kind." - **Henry James.**

Someone that is aggressive puts others around him in fear and makes them to be in a perceived danger. The same applies to a relationship when one person is such an aggressive partner, the other is in danger. He shouts at you all the time; shows a grimace, always holding you to show he is angry. Does he threaten you with violence? Do you always feel that you will pay for every wrong action of yours? This person loses his anger on every little thing, raising his voice always? These are dangerous signs in a relationship, that likely show that such a partner is aggressive. Maybe you are tempted to think that this person is still such a wonderful person with many other endearing qualities as discussed in the first part of this book, this consideration is still holding you from seeing this one as a wrong choice. If these aggressive attitudes are a way of life and not as a result of lingering troubles that such one has been going through, then you are as good as endangering your life. Aggressiveness goes a long way to have abusiveness, hot-tempered and wickedness as its colleagues, thereby making this person a poisonous snake to be with. Being aggressive is most times not always caused by situations; it is always inherent and as a result a very bad threat to deal with in a relationship. Imagine when you do what this partner doesn't like which you know is common, what will happen either by the persons choice of words or his action. This person likes war, so to say and you will always be the victim. Someone with this flaw doesn't easily change; rather he pretends as if he controls it. Once in a while he will lose it on you, and when the pressures of life begin to come upon the relationship how more visible violence will become. This serious flaw can't be hidden; it is just that some people have been so blinded to understand how bad this flaw is. They tend to think that this person has other good qualities, so they would accommodate him. And you want to accommodate such person and endanger your own life?

One thing you must understand in a relationship is that you will never change a person's disposition no matter how angelic you are. You can only endure and avoid situations that might trigger the person to show the flaw. People get beaten or spoken abusively on in a relationship because they have an aggressive partner, who they know is such yet they deceive themselves with the illusion that they will change such a partner. They keep getting hit, yet they keep being in love, and one day, bad news will be the next thing. It is very risky to have one who always acts like he is in a war front around you. Someone will tell you that this person has not laid his hands on her, but he keeps exhibiting those characteristics of being aggressive, and she is still in the relationship. This character goes a long way to show beastly part of the person, which endangers the other partner. Don't wait till you get hit before you recognize this person as the wrong person to be in a relationship with. Words alone can tell you that this person is aggressive in nature and should be at the war front and not in a relationship. He needs a rehab and not you, and needs to get his emotions down and not to get you down.

You still might be having double mind thinking that due to upbringing that this person will still change, another fallacy you are

YES, ONLY TO THE RIGHT PERSON

telling yourself. In fact you are in the dark in a broad daylight and this book has shed light on you this moment. Get out of that darkness and begin to see reality in the present situation, by seeing such one as not good for you. Being aggressive does not just stop at being abusive; it goes also a long way to put your emotions in danger. Yes, expect to be hurt all the times, and expect to be hit either by words or by fist. If that be the case, then of what benefit is a relationship when one has to endure it instead of enjoying it? Aggressiveness most of the times, takes over other loyal feelings one might have for someone. It overruns love and affection and goes on to perpetuate that bad you never expected. It takes you by sudden and reality always comes when the deed has already been done. Have you wondered why a person would raise his hands on someone he professes he loves? It is because this flaw will always overrun any tender feelings when it comes burning. This wrong person might be fooling you with a lot of 'I'm sorry' all the time and lots of crocodile tears and you keep thinking that you are safe and that he has changed or will change. Don't wait till it cost you what you will never change, a very big price. Another funny thing is that most aggressive partners in relationship tend to plead a lot, making the other person to feel safe; when it is so glaring that the person is not safe.

Whether you think that there is love and affection in the relationship, this person is a wrong partner and will always remain the wrong person for you. Instead of you to be beaten with the left hand and be consoled with the right hand, it is better to be alone and have nobody both at your left and your right. Why should someone always make you be in danger when you know you should feel safe? Why should someone make you be in fear when you bargained to be at peace? Why should you fear someone you ought to love? An adage says: "You have to have a very long spoon to be able to eat with the devil." But I keep correcting people to throw away that adage that it is never and will never be safe to even eat with the devil irrespective of the length of your spoon. Because the devil can as well grab that your very long spoon to use it as a weapon against you. And that goes with what we always read in a poem, 'that the best weapon against an evil person is to keep running away from the person.' If the person is north; then be ready to change your location to west; if possible, don't have a location at all so that you will have no tracking point.

So while this person is noticed to always exhibit this aggressiveness, irrespective of the person he has shown it toward, it is also best for you to take to your heels for your own safety. As mentioned earlier, it is glaring when one is an aggressive type; one can never hide it since it is a constant occurrence. It is not something that happens once in a while, it happens every now and then that you are with the person. Stories have it that those who have paid dearly with their life in an abusive relationship never received the abuse once or just twice. They kept getting abused by words; then it deteriorated to grabbing their arms by force and then poking in their face. Gradually it went on to fisticuff, kicking and finally to using weapon. Real love should be exactly the opposite of this in a real relationship coming from the right person who will constantly take into consideration not just your physical wellbeing but also emotional wellbeing. On no account should one be deceived that aggressiveness is not really a problem when a partner shows love. Even if the person shows the most wonderful love to you, bear it in mind that your life is in danger with such a person.

You need to be safe in a relationship and not be with the wrong person who will at all times lose his temper shouting on you and grabbing your wrist. What you need is someone that will say lovely words into your ears and not shout his voice into your ears. You need someone that will hold you tight in his arms and not grabbing your arms. Kindness is what a real relationship needs and not harshness, to be able to thrive. And even if some tells you he loves you but with a very harsh tone, then let yourself know that this person is not the right person to be with. The sad truth remains that most people who are aggressive tend to be wicked or act wickedly toward others. And no

YES, ONLY TO THE RIGHT PERSON

one will like to have a partner that is either wicked or that acts wickedly.

Sign 10

Being Restrictive

"Don't go there. Hey do it this way. Do you know why I say all these? It's because I own you like I own my car and will make use of you the way I make use of my properties."
- O.D. Chimex.

Humans are free moral agents, and as such should be allowed to choose freely and make decisions freely so far as it will not be detrimental to others. This makes us happy and makes life adventurous and fun. Imagine when this wonderful privilege is taken away from you directly or indirectly in the name of relationship. Realities begin to dawn on you that everything you do has to have a limit and this limit is set by the other person you are in a relationship with. And just like a property, you are owned and used by another person. This owner goes on to give you conditions with stringent attachments. You are being kept under control as if someone is stalking you, trailing all your movements. You are feeling the pressure since you started having contact with this person that a better part of you have been restricted from doing something which you know is not bad. Some will go a long way to tell you by words where to go and not to go, what to do and what not to do, and how to do things, you will be ordered around at will. How else will you define such a restrictive relationship,

YES, ONLY TO THE RIGHT PERSON

other than the wrong one, with someone likely not going to make a right partner?

Only kids should be restricted due to their naivety in knowing the consequences of their actions, which often results in their harm. As for adult, doing just that amounts to hostage and loss of freedom which should not be of in this modern era. Sadly the same hostage plays in many relationships, though in a very subtle way not likely that of children. Your freedom is restricted, yet you are not held in one place. You are in a relationship and not in cage and only a right person will see it that way. This danger sign in a relationship are so subtle that many will not likely call it restriction, they will call it love. You are an adult and not a kid and should be allowed to just be yourself the way you were before the relationship. Your movement shouldn't be dictated and your whereabouts shouldn't be sort for all the time. But to this wrong person, you are wrong, you are in a cage called relationship and you are a kid and not an adult. If that be the case, then why waste your time with a kidnapper, someone who will like restrict your movement by all means, treating you more like an employee?

This is one of the danger signs that a person with this attitude shows, making you look more like he owns you. He likes to keep you under control either by words or by actions, making you feel like you are a property. Nobody should own you, you should own yourself. Often, such restrictions are manifest when a partner is wealthy and has spent lots of money on the other person, and this gives this wrong person the feeling that he has bought you. Those gifts he showers you with make him to feel he has the right of ownership over you, in fact patent right. The right person will not act this way, no matter how much he has spent on you materially or emotionally. No matter how much he has spent on your family, he will never act like he owns you, if he really loves you.

Often, this attitude doesn't come in the way the person being restricted knows about it, it might come subtly, like being constantly checked on. You might not understand what is really happening to you until you finally lose your freedom, being totally controlled by another person. He keeps giving excuses as to why you need to go there and not there. He gives you excuses as to why you need to report your activities to him; and makes you think that those calls you receive are not necessary. Some go further even to remind your family members that you should be answerable to him at all times. He keeps telling you who to associate with and who not to associate with. Where you are at the moment are sort for, and the reason for going there too, you must provide. "Who are you with?" That is part of the questions you will always be conversant with because you will always answer it often.

He tries to make you think that you don't really need those people around you and that you don't really need to go certain places. These are very bad signs that this person is not likely the right person you should seek to develop a relationship with. It is never love to restrict an adult from doing what he thinks he wants to do, so far it is not harmful. Even if it is harmful, an adult should not be forced not to do anything. It is only love when you are allowed to be a free moral agent that you are, doing what gives you joy so far as it does not endanger anybody. A relationship should allow you your freedom and never take it away from you, indirectly. If you chose not to do some certain things, due to your partner; then it should be your own decision and it is love that should motivate you. And, that a partner does not do some certain things should not make him to restrict you in doing those things, as long as those things are not bad.

Take for instance, the freewill humans received from God to do whatever pleases them, within a boundary, but with caution and wisdom. That shows love for someone, and that makes humans happy. This person trying to restrict you and make you feel like you were in a cage really doesn't have a real love for you; rather this person is just

YES, ONLY TO THE RIGHT PERSON

selfish trying to protect his interest. Tell me why you won't be having problems with this person anytime you go against his restrictions? This is why it is wisdom on your part to begin to recognize this one as someone likely to be the wrong type. The other day, I was having a conversation with a lady, and she told me how often her boyfriend calls to make sure she is where she is supposed to be. She went on to say that this person always tries to give her reason not to go where she wants to or visits people she wants to. The lady told me point blank that she was fed up with that attitude of her boyfriend. I felt her plight and felt pity for her too, because she was likely with the wrong person. I imagined the plights of so many other people who are in a relationship like hers, being restricted.

To say that those people in such relationship are blindfolded is just the perfect word to use to describe their situation. Tell me how you will be happy when someone who professes love for you tries to dictate your schedule? Every of your movement should be reported, and the same goes on with all your activities, and you think you are safe with this kind of person? You are really not safe and this person is actually telling you that he is the wrong person just that you don't want to heed to the warning. What are you still waiting for to leave this person, if you have on several occasions tried to let him know that you want your freedom and it still occurs? The more you stay with this wrong person, the more you will find yourself in a cage, just like an animal; and the more you keep losing your freeness as a human. You might not really know it is a cage; the person might make it look more of a game reserve thereby making you think that you are free, whereas you are not. Then if you are not that convinced that he is restrictive, try and create a scenario where you will paint a picture of you being in the midst of others, you will see that this person will always not give you that needed support. Unless you will agree to go in his company, then you will see him giving you that support. What other way to describe this than sheer selfishness, not minding your happiness and wellbeing.

The more you try to pay deaf ear to this warning, the more you will understand that he is becoming a tyrant, restricting you the more. And the more you struggle to make him understand that you really need your freedom, the more the relationship will be saddled with troubles. And when these continuous quarrels set in, you will as well lose mental and emotional freedom. These losses are very detrimental to your wellbeing; it will cause you your happiness. That you are in a relationship does not deprive you keeping friends and being in the company of others; this your partner must understand. And when that person fails to understand this axiom, then the person is likely the wrong person to be in a relationship with.

Sign 11

Physical Appearance is the Reason for Loving

"You keep laying emphasis on the way someone looks outside, because that is the only thing you see."
- O.D. Chimex.

You might be wondering how this could make someone a wrong person to be in a relationship with. Yes, it is in fact one of the most clear and first danger sign that a wrong person always exhibits, if you are observant enough in a relationship. This person always harps on your appearance, making you know how much your beauty is making him to love you the more. Your body shape, every of your physical attributes, this person always cite as the reason for this love. The more you spend time with him, the more he tells you prompt and plain that without your physical appearance, that you would not have been his partner. He doesn't and will never tell you those good qualities that endear you to him, because there is none. What bothers him is just your body that he wants and nothing else. If your appearance is the only thing a person is interested in and sees, then why deceive yourself that he wants a relationship? You are just perfect, physically in his eyes, and that physical appearance is the only basis for this love. That is really wrong, and does make a relationship fail sooner or later. Right relationship with the right person goes beyond physical appearance; it is based on deep feelings that develop as a result of knowing that this person is different from others. Real love goes beyond the skin to look into those inner you that will make you both to want to be together. Physical appearance fades away but the inner person becomes better by the day, and only the right person who means business understands this. If that same appearance that made him notice you, is the same appearance that is making him to love you, then one day it is very likely that he will switch over to another person with better appearance than you. You need to get things straight to avoid fallen prey to a weasel.

Now sit down to analyze the way you are being praised by this person, your eyes, your voluptuous figure, the way you talk, the way you walk, and these, all the time. He has never told you that you have such a wonderful personality? Danger is lurking around you. What if something happens and some of those physical attributes are lost? Then the relationship will have to be suspended; this, the person is telling you. Although one might sometimes always sight how beautiful a partner is, but that should not be the main reason for loving this person. A right person with right intentions will always tell you how wonderful you are as a person, character-wise. Mind you that if physical appearance should be someone's reason for loving you; he will one day see reason to be fed up with your physical appearance. A right person and one who is very serious about starting a relationship looks beyond this physical attributes and he will always not lay emphasis on your physical appearance. That is the reason you see flirts going after good looking people, even if they are in the car, they will, if possible jump out of the car to woo that next beautiful person. That is the only thing they want, and that is the only thing they see as well. And those flirts that go after people with superb appearance end up wanting just to sleep with the person. But a right person will just take deep notice of you maybe by just a single display of a very rare quality or courtesy. Your

YES, ONLY TO THE RIGHT PERSON

appearance catches his fancy, but your personality moves him to want to have a relationship with you. Think now if you could remember a couple that have lived happily for like two decades or more; if you have your time go close and ask them how they met or what attracted them. The question you will get will be simple; their attraction was based on sterling personalities of both. Most times, at the initial stage one person was not interested in the other, but just that wonderful personality, he got enticed. And that is what a relationship should be based on and not just physical appearance.

If you are still confused about this person, why not kindly ask this person what attracts him to you. Then watch him and listen as he answers from his heart, with gestures, words and tone, you will come to understand. And if seventy person of what he said is on your physical appearance, you better start to distance yourself from this wrong person who is just there to appease his eyes and satisfy just a selfish motive. As he talks, the few times he will mention about your personality, he will not sound it convincingly with enthusiasm. But any word related to your physical appearance he harps on it with gestures, to show you how importantly he has placed values on them more than your personality. This is the reason you will find it rare to see those who are in a relationship with physically challenged partners to break up easily. If they are ten of them, eight will likely marry and live happily. The magic is simple; they found love and not appearance.

A wrong person will always be attracted to you because of your appearance and this, will constantly tell you indirectly or directly. Someone with serious intentions will get to like starting a relationship with you based on your personalities; this also will form his basis for loving you. It is like one wanting to get into the university to study. This person knowing that this venture will decide his future, will not go out there to choose the institution just because the compound has the best landscape with alluring flower beds and trees. A reasonable person goes beyond what are seen outside; those things that might be locked up inside the buildings are more important to him. The person may as well go beyond the number of graduates the institution churns out; to the achievements made by those graduates. Looking into the society to see how those graduates fare shows more of insight on the part of the person making that enquiry. Same with relationship, reasonable ones look beyond the physical appearance and looking into things that might likely be unseen, but felt greatly.

One who lays emphasis more on physical appearance than characters and qualities when making a choice, is somehow seen as one without wisdom, even in general aspect of life. Yes this person lacks wisdom and is bound to always make mistakes in almost every little thing he does. Ask this person to make a choice on anything; he will definitely go with ones with best looks and not one with best make and quality. This characterizes the way children make their judgment, because they lack the wisdom. Assuming that you are with this person that lays too much emphasis on appearance, maybe, eating out in a restaurant; and one with a better appearance than you, passes by, you will be embarrassed the way he will be ogling at that person. He is just having his certificate of stupidity and he goes around displaying it, but you might not be observant enough to read it.

When one keeps telling you that he loves you just because you are appealing to his eyes; the same person will as well leave you when he thinks that you are no longer appealing. Why not take your time and check out if this person has this danger sign and then find your way before you will be shown an exit door by this person. Such person is simply telling you that he wants your appearance and not you, and gradually you will see him make known his intentions about wanting just your body. To him, everything you do is perfect and he finds it hard to correct you even when you should be corrected. This will show you that he is not interested in building a relationship with you, but interested in building on your body. He might sometimes not really want to see the inner you, because he will not likely want to make you

YES, ONLY TO THE RIGHT PERSON

a better person. Don't let this person try to sweep you off your feet with words, painting you perfect physically. A serious minded person who wants to start and build a relationship will at all times love you due to your personality, and this he will always be letting out.

Sign 12

Belittles You

"Keep away from those who try to belittle your ambitions. Small people always do that, but the really great make you believe that you too can become great."
- Mark Twain.

As a kid, I saw people who belittled others as just entertainers that liked cracking jokes a lot. But as I grew older, it became glaring that those people that belittle others especially in public have no real affection for the ones they belittle. Someone who belittles you in essence is dismissing you as unimportant, and that is the way he wants the public to also see you. If that be the case, then why should someone be fond of belittling his partner especially in public, either with friends, colleagues, relatives and others? A very clear sign that this person is either not the right person or that he values you not. Having deep respect for someone goes a long way to be demonstrated not just by words, but by the way such person sees and takes the one he respects, within his heart. The value he places on the person as well as the way he projects such a person outside, says more of the love he has for you. That you are being referred to as a darling all the time is not just enough to prove that someone values you. What makes it enough is when someone proves and shows others that you are a darling, even at your

YES, ONLY TO THE RIGHT PERSON

back. No matter how a clown someone is, if he is the right person, he will never make fun of you when with others.

Assuming that this person calls you all wonderful names, but always tells others or insinuate to others that you are worthless; shows he has no deep regard for you in his heart. Gradually you notice that he always puts you down when either in public or private. The more you try to see it as a joke the more he makes it glaring that, it is for real. Not just by words, the actions also show that you are being looked down upon. This is no joke, you are being dismissed as worthless and that is what you will remain for the rest of the relationship, as long as it lasts. And if a person sees you as worthless, tell me how possible such one will ever respect you and your feelings? You begin to wonder when this person will stop making fun of you; only when he starts valuing you. The fact remains that when a partner constantly makes fun of you either in public or in private, there is every chances that he will as well be washing your dirty linens outside. This washing spans across telling others your weaknesses and mistakes.

This might be an attitude one has developed over the years, but then it is very bad and shows lack of deep respect for someone in a relationship. The same way he addresses you with mockery choice of words is likely the same way he will discuss you with others, and that is the way he sees you in his heart. What one may see as a joke might not sound as one to another person, and only intelligent people understand this. Then if that be the case, why not this partner take your feelings into consideration and avoid making you look unimportant most of the time? Even when jokes are made, must it be to put you down always? Must it be to make others laugh at you, whereas he should be making others to respect you? This wrong person will never understand how bad he projects you, because you are worth nothing to him. He makes you worth less when you are in public and talks to you in a manner he likes even if you say otherwise. The more he does it, the more your self-respect diminishes and the more others see you as one that is so unimportant.

With words alone, someone can tell what value he places on another person. There is this adage that says: "A wise person does not call his boat a scrap. If he does so, others will come into the boat with garbage." Even if there is a cause to crack joke with what mistake one has done, must it be in public? Must the choice of words be mockery? This wrong person does not want to understand this, and cares not if you are a laughing stock in the public. So far as he feels comfortable to laugh while you get angry, he gives no damn. And that is the highest point of selfishness which should not be so in a relationship; you matter not to him. It is love when one paints your wrong as right in public, but lovingly corrects you in private. It is love when he tells others that you are worth their respect and they see you that way. But if he continues to insinuate that you are such a dumb, then people will not hesitate to take you by his words.

This belittling is in the heart and not merely on the lips. Before one makes words, he must have seen a connection between the things he compares. If he likens you to an animal, then he is as well saying that you have some characteristics of that animal. The bad side of it is that one that belittles you often times do it in public as well. In fact most of them do it at your back, while you are not there to put a defense for yourself. Like a joke, this person discusses with a stranger, a colleague, and a relative about you and your flaws, simply because he doesn't value you and cares nothing about how your reputation will be battered. I sit down and listen with pity for the victim, when their partners come to me to discuss the flaws of the other person. This person calls it complain, but it is absolutely wrong to tell others the flaws of your partner if you really value such person. It shows lack of love and deep respect for the other person. It again shows stupidity on the part of that person that tells the flaws of the other partner to outsiders. So why would you still want to have dealings with someone lacking sense.

YES, ONLY TO THE RIGHT PERSON

"Look, my partner is stupid." That is what this person is saying in essence. And we all know that it takes a stupid person to associate with a stupid person, "birds of a feather flock together," they say. So this person is telling others that he is stupid to have a stupid partner. And this boils down to one being in a relationship with someone lacking wisdom.

Another thing I found about this wrong people that always belittle their partners is that they also go a long way to laugh at the mistakes of their partners in order to mock them, which is very bad. Your partner should always come in your defense even when others are against you and not supporting others to mock or laugh at you. Even though there is a cause to crack jokes with your partner, appropriate choice of words should be used and let it be clear that it is a joke, and not making it public when others are around. Joke should be made not to hurt anyone but to make anyone to laugh, and when you put others down for others to laugh, it shows lack of respect and love for those put down. A partner's stupidity should be shared by both partners and not to be left for one person to bear the brunt. You both in a relationship have just one single cross to bear; that is what makes it a relationship working together for a particular purpose. All these, the wrong person will never understand, that is more reason you have to let go of that wrong person that belittles you at will either in privately or publicly, by words or actions. Belittling is a kind of contagious thing; if you keep being around someone that finds joy in belittling others; soon you may copy this bad habit, and belittle others at will without putting their reputation into consideration.

And if a partner should affect you negatively, then that person is the wrong person and should be discarded. A right person should always see reasons to broadcast your sterling qualities and not to broadcast your flaws. Apart from those that belittle others as fun, there are those that are mean in belittling others. They tell it to your face at slightest mistakes, that you are unimportant. And you begin to wonder as well if you are not important too in the relationship, and that is what it means. Other way this wrong person might be belittling you is by his actions. Your feelings are ignored seeing it as not important, just like you are not. He treats you as if you worth no respect with disregard for your reputation. So please begin to see this person as the wrong person, if this danger sign is so glaring in the relationship. This person that belittles you all the time will one day tell it to your face that you matter not to him just like the relationship matters not to him; either by actions or by words. This attitude disintegrates you, making you feel inferior and inadequate for him. And don't be surprised that sooner or later you will find out that others will be looking down on you; because your partner has told them that you are just not important, exposing just your flaws. You are worth more only in the eyes of the right person.

Sign 13

Sweet Words Start Immediately

"The devil can cite scripture for his purpose."

- William Shakespeare.

The moment it occurred to me to add this very danger sign to this list, I guffawed. The reason is that lots of people are either guilty of this particular thing or have fallen prey. Because of the human nature, honeyed words always sweep people off their feet; weasels and flirts have this at their fingertips to prey on naïve ones. You may have in one way or the other sweet-tongued someone making the person do what he ordinarily wouldn't have done. It might be that you have heard experiences of people that had sweet-tongued others making them fell for their charm in one time or the other. As humans, it pleases us to hear what makes our heart to gladden, what can lift our spirit up and make us feel very important and wanted. Whether young or old, you could be a victim of this hoodwinking. This fact, the wrong person always takes advantage of, and before you know it, you are already taken off your feet. Imagine when you barely know someone for just hours or days or few weeks and this person has started gushing about you, promising to give you heaven and earth. The very first time he comes closer to you, he has started gushing how you look prettier than angels. How perfect you are and how you are just like a goddess. This person just requested for your number and each time he calls, he spends minutes showering you with praises, giving you all sorts of romantic sobriquet as names. What about those texts he sends you? Look at the texts, the darlings and sweethearts are more than the actually thing he wants to say. To you, this person is such a sweet person; but to the person, you are just a prey. Why he does this is to weaken your defenses and hold your emotions at ransom.

At first, the naïve one will be flying above the sky in ecstasy not knowing that this flight is a kamikaze. In your mind, you have met the most amazing person in the world, making you feel priceless with words. But no, this person is just a wrong person and this is one of the signs that he has come to swindle you of your heart and feelings. No matter how right one will become in a relationship, just hours and days and weeks are not enough to come to a conclusion how sweet this person will be. Real love grows like a seed, and this proximity is not enough to grow a long lasting relationship that will stand the test of time. As mentioned in the opening part of this topic, everyone has either fallen victim to this trick or has in one way or the other used it on someone, though it might not really be relationship related. I have seen myself in both sides; first, I will talk about using those sweet words on someone. The reason then was not as a result of being a weasel but out of naivety, I used it to get a girl fall in love. That kind of love was not envisaged to mature to serious commitment; I knew that, due to the age. Then, letter writing was very common and as the simplest means of getting to woo a girl. I could remember how I searched the dictionary, bought some romantic pamphlets that gave tips on all sorts of coined sweet words, to make the potential person reading the letter to be mesmerized. And it worked perfectly on the victim then. Second, I could as well remember the first time I got a letter from a girl expressing her interest on me with superb sweet words. Imagine each night I had to read the letter and smiled myself to sleep. Sweet words

YES, ONLY TO THE RIGHT PERSON

actually will have effect on you if you don't cut this wrong person from making your emotions a puppet.

As you get to let this person in, you will find out that these sweet praises will continue without let up, because he only wants to hold your emotions at ransom. You might think that by your age that you are above being sweet-tongued. Really it knows no age boundary and knows no status. This person is just like that bird catcher that will scatter baits few inches away from a trap till it leads to that death zone of the trap. The more he spews the words and you take them in, the closer you will become on being his prey. He wants to make you a puppet and you are insensitive enough to see this person as a wrong person. Gradually your senses, your feelings and your heart will be getting closer to that trap and by the time you will get to know what actually is happening, you have already been caught. Then it becomes too difficult to let go of this wrong person having you in his custody. The more you try to break away from this person, the more those sweet words already said and sweet empty promises keep drawing you down. Everything he says records in your memory and you take it that way. How else will you describe someone that is just serious about making you a slave emotionally, just to fulfill his selfish desire?

This danger sign needs to be taken seriously because this is the clearer and the first sign that will manifest when this person is coming with a wrong motive. How could someone who barely knows you, begin to refer to you as his wife, if not that he wants to dislodge your defenses? How could someone that should still be studying you, conclude that you are such a perfect person for him? He goes on to promise you heaven and earth, taking you round the world, and will show you the moon. And you think he is for good? This does not mean that sweet words should not be used in a relationship. Here is making it point-blank that when these hyper sweet words and promises become the start of a relationship; then the person vomiting it is likely coming with an ulterior motive, to exploit you. One who is serious about a relationship that will lead to real commitment will not be eager to get you held down with words and promises. This is because if you happen to prove to be the wrong person, then he can as well find his way. And reasonableness on his part makes him not to hold your emotions down, while the assessment goes on.

The start of a good relationship is like a test-driving period, where one involved should take it easy and not make the whole thing happen too fast. This person making you go down on your knees with words and promises is really a dangerous person, but you don't get to see him that way. To you, he says what gladdens your heart and at the same time, blinding you with those sweet words. A real person wanting to go into a relationship should see it as college where one goes into to study and come out with a degree. And that study starts gradually with lectures climaxing to exams and eventually computations of results and certification. Know this that it is only fraudulent for an institution to certify you without examining you, if it happened that way, then the institution remains the wrong one.

So if one who barely knows you and wants to get to know better starts to give you a certificate of pass when you have not taken any examination; A's and no B's or C's, then you are in with the wrong person. The best thing to do is to reject the results and quit that person. You will marvel that this person that you think you meant heaven and earth to will not give a damn when you finally take a walk. This is because he sees you as a bad business and has no time to go back on a failed business. If one thinks that he will only impress you by words and by promising you heaven and earth, then his intentions will likely be business oriented, to also impress you. He invests those things simply because he wants to have a profit sooner or later. And that profit is nothing than taking advantage of you, to exploit your feelings. The same way a devil will quote a Scripture just to achieve his aim of deceit is the same way this person will make promises just to make sure that his selfish motives are achieved.

Sign 14

Does Not Yield

"I'm unpredictable; I never know where I'm going until I get there. I'm so random, I'm always growing, learning, changing; I'm never the same person twice. But one thing you can be sure of about me is, I will always do exactly what I want to do." - **C. JoyBell C.**

At a young age maybe, you were meant to understand by some of your parents' actions, that being an adult means standing by your words and not making a move no matter how the pressure is. Though quite good for parents in instilling discipline into their kids; sadly, it becomes a danger sign when it is glaring in a relationship. Understanding the word yielding is very important especially the role it plays in a relationship. Giving way to demand or pressure from a partner when no issue of right or wrong is at stake tends to be a wonderful quality any relationship needs, especially when the man exhibits it. It is also very wonderful when any of the partners sees that the course he is pursuing is bringing a trouble and that surrendering to the pressure for the sake of peace will not be detrimental. But what if this is lacking in your partner? This is another real sign that he might really not be the kind of partner that will make you happy; he is that wrong type. In order for two different people to come together and achieve a meaningful relationship, they must be ready to give way to pressure or demand. And in order for a partner to always make you happy in a relationship, he must be ready to give way to pressure when it becomes intense.

Now look at it this way, you both have different tastes, views, opinions and will not always agree to one thing some of the times. These divergence is common and it is expected in a relationship since you both are different individuals coming together to chart a single course. But what if you have come to understand that this person is always insisting on his way, he never gives in? An issue comes up and this issue degenerates but instead of this person to mellow down for the sake of peace, he is bent, and whatever it will cost, he cares not. On several occasions you advised him and it was very clear that your advice was the only needed solution to a particular problem; again he remained adamant on changing his way. What if something happened and you begged him to change a course of action, but at last you got disappointed, he went on and did it just like he had wanted. These are some of the dangerous displays of one not ready to yield, and this particular sign goes with only the wrong person. It only shows that such a person is a diehard stubborn fellow. Relationship with someone like this only goes on to hurt you all the time. Plead with this person till tomorrow; he makes no move until he does it the way he wants. This is selfishness which should be unheard of in a relationship, and it destroys relationship quick.

Think deep into the future when issues and pressures will be arising, and instead of this person to surrender for the sake of peace, he will be bent to see to the last part of the issue. He simple shows that he is rigid, and mostly people that are rigid are very difficult to please and to deal with. They are always proud people who think that only their way, deeds, and thinking are just the perfect. Tell me how you will cope with one who finds it difficult to keep pace with the world of changes? Someone who finds it hard to make amendments in order to

YES, ONLY TO THE RIGHT PERSON

carry everybody along in the relationship? And this will hurt you seriously if you continue to have a relationship with such person. Though, one should not be so flexible like a chameleon changing at every giving moment. And again, one should not always be man pleaser, just to let peace reign; that is not what we are talking about. We are talking about one not yielding when there is every good reason to do that; when there is pressure that will likely be worse if left to continue. It shows a lot of respect to allow other people's reasonable views to take place instead of yours. And this, this wrong person is finding very difficult to understand. You might think that this does not really matter in a relationship, but it matters a lot, stubbornness breaks relationship, frustrating the other partner. One who does not yield simply means that he doesn't put others into consideration and this person invariably is saying that he is not a person of peace. Tell me why a right person will be bent on a particular course at the expense of the other person? Only a selfish person thinks in this direction and one who is very selfish, will always be a wrong person to be in a relationship with.

You might think that a particular gender is meant to be rigid, but that is not always the truth; any of the genders could be. For the sake of peace and love, one must at various points in time, mellow down for other. Yielding is a very good quality in a relationship and in family too. Take for instance, no matter how tough a parent might be he yields when necessary, sometimes when a child's view needs to be taken into consideration. That does not make such a parent weak, but it shows love, a love ready to surrender for another to be happy. Partners in a relationship should really be ready, and have that spirit to always surrender when doing so will not be detrimental. And one without this quality invariably is saying that he is the wrong person to be with. This is why you might sometimes hear a partner complaining bitterly about being in a relationship with a stubborn person. He goes on to continue to endure and complain about this unyielding attitude of the other person. And complains go with being unhappy in a relationship; I am sure you wouldn't want that. This person will continue to have his way and not letting the other person's feelings to count. This yielding is actually as a result of pressures coming from the other party, and this person being the wrong person will be bent on his course till that pressure turns into a big issue disintegrating the relationship.

Someone with an unyielding spirit somehow says that he will never concede to defeat, and one exhibiting such spirit in a relationship says in essence that this is a battle field where supremacy is the issue. Wherever there is relative peace in a relationship, there must a man of peace and that man of peace is nobody than a person yielding when the pressure becomes much. Some of the troublesome in a relationship is as a result of this unyielding attitude of a partner. Nobody wants to submit or surrender for the sake of peace and that makes issues to rise and rise till it climaxes, making both parties to be worse off. Yielding really shows that such a person is wise; he has envisioned the future and saw a calamity and then proceeded to conceal himself. But a foolish person ends up being myopic, seeing just within; and nobody will like to have a relationship with a foolish person.

This danger sign when seen in person makes the person a rigid person to be in a relationship with and rigidity always brings about conflicts upon conflicts that will likely break a relationship. Take for instance, we live in a dynamic world and one seems to be rigid, the person will definitely be coming in conflict with the changing realities on ground. More reason you should take your time and get to watch this person whether he exhibits this attitude of not yielding when the pressure becomes tense, and that yielding will not be detrimental. This wrong person cares not what happens; he only cares about his ego, and not what will result from that particular hell bent attitude. Funny, this stubborn person that exhibits this attitude will never do it that way that is supposed to benefit the other party to a relationship, and he gives no damn. Someone stubborn does not take into consideration other

YES, ONLY TO THE RIGHT PERSON

person's feeling; he will even bother not if that particular course hits the rock, so far as that his decision is allowed to happen. His happiness is not just on seeing a course succeed, but on seeing that his words come to pass, jut to protect his ego. A partner who will be ready to relinquish possession of something, decision or opinion for the sake of peace, is what you want. And only such person will always be putting you into consideration in all matters; no other person will do that except the right person.

Sign 15

Being Manipulative

"The beginning of love is to let those we love be perfectly themselves, and not to twist them to fit our own image. Otherwise we love only the reflection of ourselves we find in them." - **Thomas Merton.**

The first time I set my eyes on Mr. Benson and his wife, I saw a perfect match; couple who were compatible. But as time went on, I began seeing a marriage being manipulated by another person. His wife began to exhibit characters that showed she had her husband at her fingertips, making him do whatever she wants even at the expense of the man and his family members. This manipulation was not by force; the man did all she wanted him to do willingly, but to his own detriment. I watched this man drove away his niece and brought in almost all his wife's siblings to live with them. Benson's mother seldom visits Benson, whereas his wife's mother lived with them. This manipulation began to manifest outside their home, Benson became more of a moron, wanting his wife to participate in all his affairs including taking decision for him. I lived with Benson and his family in the same neighborhood. Similar scenario plays in many relationships, and the end is always disastrous. Manipulation though seems subtle and unimportant, it weighs heavily on relationship. The partner that is

YES, ONLY TO THE RIGHT PERSON

manipulative always tends to plunge the other person into doom. In some parts of the world, people attribute this to a spell, insinuating that one partner is bewitching the other. But in most cases, it has often been as a result of one partner being manipulative. If a person shows this kind of manipulative spirit, likely he may not make a good partner; such a person is always cunning.

This person subtly makes you do things that ordinarily you wouldn't have done, and you find it difficult to come to understand that this is manipulation. Often times, he coerces you to do things against your wish, unscrupulously influencing you. You might call it love but in the actual sense your partner is exercising unscrupulous control over you. Rather than doing it in a forceful way, this person resorts to using emotions to play down on your intelligence making you change your course almost at the eleventh hour. Relationship should be left open, a level playing ground where nobody is coerced wrongly by the other for selfish purpose. It is very difficult sometimes to notice this bad sign, especially if this person is tactical. Come to think of that moment when you want to do something and suddenly you find yourself doing it the other way just to please the other person. Think of that moment when he wants to influence every little thing that you do even decisions and choices concerning you as a person. This is not love but a danger sign that he might end up turning you to a slave in the relationship. The reason this influence is not coming with force is that you have no commitment with this person. As soon as serious commitment is made, like engagement or marriage, then you will come to understand how forceful and authoritative this influence will be. He wants to control you at every moment that is why he manipulates you, making you think it is love.

The one manipulating you is not doing that in your own interest, he is just doing it for his own selfish interest. Think that experience narrated at the opening paragraph about Benson, his wife practically and tactically distanced his relatives and siblings from him thereby bringing her own family in. Imagine the amount of other negative result that would come out of her manipulation; too bad that it affected Benson's relationship with his neighbours and business partners. Virtually everybody in the neighborhood distanced himself from him, because they knew that everything he does he must bring his wife in. This wrong person manipulating you has ulterior motive and that ulterior motive is not for your own good or for the good of the relationship. It is just for his good alone at your expense, in a subtle way. He wants to keep you just in a cage letting you out with an invisible rope tied on your neck to take you around when you want to go out. Those pleadings, necking and pecking, to do it the way he likes, you really have to give it a deeper thought; it might be signs of manipulation. He knows that what he wants you to do might be unscrupulous and that is the reason he comes subtly with coercion to make you succumb. The same way he makes you do what only pleases him, will be the same way he will one day make you eat dung just because it pleases him as well. Watch when you begin to do things exactly the way a partner wants and not the way you want and know will be the best. Will you want a partner who always holds your emotions at ransom simply because he wants you to do the way it pleases him? Such a relationship is likely going to be one-sided, one person being exploited.

Consequences of this manipulation are always gravely; not only that you will be a puppet, you will also be dependently stupid to always make mistake in your decisions. This is as a result of constant maneuvering in order to suit the will of this person. You will keep being tensed up until this partner approves anything you do; if not you will continue to be at a loggerhead with him. Your career might suffer too along the line, your business might go as well and your relationship with people will be severed, without you knowing. This wrong person exhibiting this danger sign cares not what will be the outcome of that manipulation, so far as it benefits him alone, you go to hell. You might think that you are very principled and that you don't compromise

YES, ONLY TO THE RIGHT PERSON

standard, wait till you meet a person that is manipulative. You will continue to act stupidly and compromise standards till you are doomed, and that is final. In some relationships, manipulative partner continues to influence the other person, milking the person till he goes dry. That is why you see lots of people changing to something else immediately they go into relationship; manipulation may have set in.

That wonderful treatment that you never have gotten from this person, but as soon as he wants you to do something to suit him he comes up with it, making you go by his dictates. He wants you to buy him another car, and not too long you just bought him a car; that week alone you will be treated like an angel. Hit this person severally, call him idiot countless times, you will always be right till that car comes in, then you will be ready to pay for those sins you committed before buying that car. You think it is love? It is only love when you are allowed by your partner to express yourself and not lording it over himself to dictate for you. He has a goal; and that goal is to use you to climb, making you active but dormant. I see the reason most people use that phrase, "drunken in love." Really one person is drunk and one who is drunk always does what he will not do when he is in his right senses. And this he will willingly be doing without taking notice of what he is doing. Do not let this happen to you, don't give this wrong person that chance to be in your life, it will do you more harm than good. This sign diffuses like a gas till it fills a particular place without anyone seeing it. You can only perceive it if you are observant enough. Just like this gas, it is combustible and the fire is deadly. One who really loves you will; never want to influence you unscrupulously, making you do it just the way he wants to his benefit. The right person will always come straight; and not beaten about the bush to achieve an unreasonable plan.

Don't be fooled to believe this is love; this is practically a danger sign that will be very insidious in a relationship. You will hurt lots of people if you stay in a relationship with a manipulative person. Such a person will end up making you enemy with your friends, and your relatives. This wrong person continues to pitch you against yourself to your own detriment and to his gain. Instead of being manipulative, a right person will only be supportive putting your interest first in anything he does. A manipulative person will always be deceptive tricking you into thinking that any course of action you change along the line, the way he wants, will benefit you; not knowing he will be the only beneficiary from such action. You will continue to be the loser in all the deals, while such manipulative one becomes the gainer.

Sign 16

Being Possessive

"Relationship is like sand held in your hand. Held loosely, with open hand, the sand remains where it is. The minute you close your hand and squeeze tightly to hold on, the sand trickles through your fingers. You may hold onto some of it, but most will be spilled. A relationship held loosely, with respect and freedom for the other person, it is likely to remain intact. But hold too tightly, too possessively, and the relationship slips away and is lost." - **Kaleel Jamison.**

On daily activities of humans, they always show the traits of wanting to have anything full and they derive satisfaction doing that. But same thing when applied into relationship backfires. At some point in time, you will understand that it is in human nature to have possession of something, to a degree. But then, this should only be with regards to property alone; this, lots of people don't understand. Although regarding property, one that is always too possessive, always ends up endangering his life. This person can go beyond miles in order to stupidly protect that which he has a possessive attitude toward. And this type of protection goes a long way to distress that which is being protected. He might have as many as he doesn't need, but will still not be happy to see one of them in another person's possession. This person has more than six cars lying idle, but will not let one of the idle cars be made use by another person that is in need of car. If that be the case, how much more when that car is just one, then he might kill to let people not come closer. Imagine when one you are in a relationship begins to exhibit this danger sign. Don't you think this person is likely a wrong person to be in a relationship with? The answer is yes; such person will not make you a good partner.

He demands to have your total attention and love all the time, in fact twenty four seven; round the clock relationship, he wants you just to himself. And when you dare not give it to this person, he assumes that you are giving it to another person; too bad to have such a person as a partner. Sooner or later you will go in for it, to the extent that even to spend time with your family members or other friends will be difficult. He will continue to make you sad always, restricting you to himself alone. "Please I don't want you to leave my side." And he means it, bothering you all the time to always be by his side. To people who are naïve or relatively new in a relationship, especially the first timers, they will call it love; whereas it is another modern slavery in the form of love. Do not be fooled, it is not love rather a dangerous sign that this person will make life too difficult and sad for you in that relationship. Possessive attitude breeds trouble which is very detrimental to any relationship. As a result of this possessive attitude, several times, the news have reported situations where partners have gone to the extent of killing the child of a partner, simply because they wanted to have that person's attention selfishly alone.

This attitude goes with intense jealousy as well and bickering all the time. You have to change your timetable to suit this partner all the time; and if you really don't see this person as a wrong person you are heading for a doom. He goes to an occasion; you should accompany him irrespective of your own schedule. You dare not leave his side and as soon as you do, barrages of calls inundate you. He acts as if his life

YES, ONLY TO THE RIGHT PERSON

depends on you, and that if you leave, that he will die. Being in a relationship does not mean that any other friendship with other people will not exist. It should exists, only that it should be left on a platonic level; but this, this wrong person is finding difficult to understand. He goes on with this possessiveness to distract and disrupt you all the time, making you to always change course when you really don't want to. The more you try to let him give you a space, the more you find him wanting to have the whole of you more and often, because you have become his opium. How will you then make out time to do other things that will be beneficial and make you happy? This is the kind of question you have to be given a serious thought anytime your partner begins to exhibit this act of possessiveness.

Though this person might not always make you feel being forced, but he will always be pissing you off by doing things that will always whip up your emotions anytime you don't oblige his request of being his all the time. Imagine what it will always take you emotionally when you try to make him see the reason to allow you space and this person insists that you are just hurting him by not being always around him. And each time you say no, you will be feeling guilty for not obliging his unreasonable and selfish request. How on earth you will be happy in a relationship when one tries to hold you down and then accuses you of wrong doing when you know actually that you are not guilty? If care is not taken, a partner being this possessive will go a long way to hunt the other person when he quits; if such a person allows the relationship with such one to become serious. For this reason, you have to take a walk when you just notice this danger sign in a partner, before allowing the relationship get too serious when quitting will put you in danger. This people who are so possessive are the kind of people that when they are deeply in love with someone, and their partner break up, they consider suicide as the only solution. Will it be wise on your part to allow this wrong person to fall deeply in love with you, putting himself on the suicide watch list?

O.D. CHIMEX

The disguising thing is that he might not be aggressive at this starting level of the relationship, because you have no commitment with him. But think of when you finally settle down with this person, then, you must and will understand that you are owned like a property. If one could actually feel he owns you when you are just a friend, it is obvious that he will be worse when commitment is made. I could remember my personal experience with a lady. This lady became so possessive that she wanted us to do almost everything together. Oh my goodness, she was like, "I am traveling do you mind traveling with me? I want to go this place, why not go that same place so that we could meet and be together? It is Saturday, I wanted to go for a walk, why not join me let us walk together." The more I tried to do the other way, the more I found out that she got hurt and I spent most of those little trying time, pleading, instead of studying her. I kept changing my schedule as she demanded, and when I failed to, I became the one hurting her. She took no time of mine into consideration. I lost my freedom mentally and physically and at the same time felt guilty always, thinking that I hurt her. That situation was so confusing then for me; but you won't see it that way at the start, not until you begin feeling the impact on your emotional wellbeing.

So many other distractions you will be embarrassed with if you are in a relationship with a possessive person. You keep trying your best to make things work; to achieve a balance and this person keeps trying his own best to disorganize you, your plan and all your activities. At a time he becomes your demi-god, all you need do is to work for him all the time, just please him. This person becomes an addict and you become his addiction making you both guilty of hurting each other. And at the long run the relationship will continue to head to no destination, because sooner or later, one person will be fed up. Although circumstance might warrant a person in a relationship to need the company of another person more than before, like in a situation of tragedy befallen a partner; but if that is not the case, this person is likely

YES, ONLY TO THE RIGHT PERSON

a wrong person to be in a relationship with. He will continue to be a torn in your flesh making you not to enjoy the dividends of being in a relationship. It can only be love when you are in a relationship, still have your freedom to associate with others at will, do what makes you happy, and not feel guilty that you do so. What will hurt you the most is when someone makes you his addiction using you only to satisfy his selfish motives when he feels like.

Sign 17

Being Quarrelsome

"Don't be deceived, I quarrel always simple because I hate peace." - O.D. Chimex.

Living in a world filled with troubles and disappointments could be very challenging, but staying in a relationship with someone that is quarrelsome is more challenging. The moment you take your mind to think deeper about this serious danger sign is the moment you will understand how serious it affects a relationship. Maybe you go meet a woman with a nagging husband to tell you the hell she goes through each day. How bad it is with this wife, and people around her, putting up with this nagging husband. Even the bible describes the situation as being better to stay on the roof of a house than staying in the same house with a quarrelsome person. This attitude is just a temperament, one does not really learn it or forced by situation to have it. It goes a long way to not only destroy a relationship, it also destroys the other party to the relationship. Think of a situation you are in a relationship with someone that likes to quarrel almost all the time, how restless you will be when you keep pleading with this person to let peace rain and he stands his ground, inflaming issues. This person will always make a point angrily, inciting disagreement and making angry arguments. Sometimes you think that he has let a bygone be bygone, you got it all

YES, ONLY TO THE RIGHT PERSON

wrong. At that point, a more serious issue is about to erupt, you will keep watching out for season two. Never ending quarrel will continue to linger in such relationship with a quarrelsome person. The more he sees you look peaceful, and the atmosphere serene, the more it hurts him, and pushes him to ignite a fire.

How on earth do you think a relationship will work when a contentious person is a party to that relationship? His doglike attitude will continue to disturb the peace of the relationship and disorganizes you at the same time. Think about that moment a dog barks at every little thing that passes by with the intention that it is doing its owner good. The tensed up feelings each barking comes with; that is exactly what a quarrelsome person thinks when he ignites fire. To him he thinks that he is doing the right thing, but that so-called right thing will be pissing off the other party involved. It is in our nature to need a conducive environment, at least a relative tranquility to be able to achieve a meaningful goal and be happy. But having someone with this danger sign beside you makes you to achieve nothing when you know that you are working hard. He keeps distracting you and the relationship until it finally packs up.

When I see a relationship where one partner is troublesome, I feel pity for the relationship and also for the other partner who is a victim. That victim is like someone that just bought and old rickety car, he will always spend most of his time and resources in the mechanic, trying to repair one fault or the other. And at the end, he ends up being stranded at the road after the repaired car must have broken down again. The more you try to repair the car, the more new faults resurface. That precious time that should be used to achieve something meaningful, you spend it trying to make peace, settling issues and calming a fuming partner down. And the moment you think you have repaired a present issue; then you will get disappointed on the road just when you don't expect it. Do you think you can cope with such a person in a relationship? Capital no is the answer; you will end up being messed up at last. Quarrelsome person has so many things making him to flare up most of the time, and those things he will never like to discuss with you. You will keep asking yourself, trying to understand why this person always gets heated up all the time. At this moment, it is just like wasting your time and resources trying to fix a rickety car, which will eventually disappoint you. You have to call it a quit with this person if you really want to be happy.

This wrong person could never be pleased; everything you do is just bad, because it is in his nature to abhor peace. Imagine when you just sacrifice something to please him and you will be told in the face that your effort amounts to nothing. If you are the male you may be forced to develop aggressiveness to counter such partner, but that will not solve the problem. Will that be the kind of person you want to be with all the time, someone that will only bring out the beast in you and undermine that angel in you? If not for anything, think of that moment you need rest, you are about to get one, all of a sudden he spoils your mood, by exhuming a buried issue. Such one never forgives easily; this unforgiving spirit in him makes him to want to quarrel all the time. Each time he wants to forgive you, that bad side of him will say no and he will spark up, triggering another round of quarrel. Will that be the kind of scenario you would like to be playing out in your relationship? This is why you should avoid such person, at least to have a peace of mind and to enjoy your rest when you want to.

Someone that is quarrelsome always bears grudge to a very high degree, he never forgets no matter how you plead with him. This person is like an excavator, always unearthing buried issues, to use it presently for attack. This reminds me of a family in the neighborhood, a couple and their three children. This man keeps late night, drinks; in fact you rarely meet him at home. People took this man as wayward, but then you will pity him if he tells you his story. At the dead nights, we will always hear voices, but in the morning, the voices went down. Nobody knew why those voices went up in the midnight and became

YES, ONLY TO THE RIGHT PERSON

faint in the early hours of the day. The big shock came and that was when the secret behind their constant quarrels was divulged. This man was found dead, his contentious wife killed him while asleep. It became known that those nights, she shouted at the man, and early in the morning, the man left the house to avoid her nagging attitude, coming back very late at night. But then as soon as she saw him in the house, she continued where she stopped. And this continued till the man got killed by that same woman.

With a quarrelsome person nagging becomes a norm and your peace is threatened, your life is in danger, even your emotions will continue to suffer most of the times. This person with such bad trait should be seen as a wrong person and not just a person who is hot-tempered. One might be hot-tempered but will only be aggressive when provoked and can as well try to be calm when there is no disagreement or issues being raised. But this quarrelsome person argues angrily anytime issues come up and will try to create a scene to start nagging you when it seems calmness has set in. He makes his point angrily, ending up disagreeing on a truce. A reasonable and right person though might not agree all the time but that will not always cause feud. And a relationship will always witness disagreement sometimes but will not be heated up. The right person each time an issue comes out; makes his point calmly and not angrily, and wants to avoid heated situations.

But this contentious person goes on and on to be destructive, destroying your life, your peace of mind and finally the relationship. The more you try to always device a way to make things better, the more he does things that will be detrimental to you and the relationship. The best and rational decision to make when you notice a partner has this danger sign, is not to endure or find a way to make the relationship work, but to walk out on the person and out of the relationship. You might not know what harm you are doing to yourself trying to stay in such relationship, until you have your peace when you are out of the relationship. Save your energy and resources to invest in the right relationship with the right person instead of wasting them in the wrong relationship with the wrong person.

Part Three
Knowing This Person Better

Introduction

*People wear a mask of lies so they look attractive, so be careful." - **Muhammad Saqib.***

Talking about qualities that would make one a right person for a relationship, and those ones that are seen as dangers signs making one a wrong person, is not just enough in making up your mind to hand over your emotions to a total stranger, so to say. It would be better to measure this person with other tools so as to be sure of whom really he is. For the fact that some people are thespians, putting up a façade, makes it very imperative to weigh this person thoroughly, more of a telescopic observation, before making this commitment. The tools with which to carry out this assessment, this section discusses extensively. These tools are also important because they magnify this person's personality exposing his real disposition. Someone might though be exhibiting the qualities of a good partner; that is not enough to conclude that he will make just a perfect match. You need to get to know this person very well so as to come to conclusion what sort of person he is. It behoves you to know your partner very well so that you don't feel regret in the future, when the person's real characters will begin to manifest. And if you are still confused and in doubt about what this person is at heart, this is the time to dowse your apprehension because you are going to read how to be sure of him. Observe this person from a different arena and be sure before you make this serious commitment. Don't be like those ones whom their partners turned out to be just like

YES, ONLY TO THE RIGHT PERSON

wrapped gifts; only to be left with regrets after they have made commitments. Make this commitment with all boldness having known who really your partner is, with the aid of this wonderful book.

Tool 1

How This Person Treats Others

"The way people treat others, is a statement about who they are as human beings. It is not a statement about you." - Bianca Bressy.

Imagine you are with this partner and he opens the door for an elderly person. At first you might not really take this as something important, not until he continues to show by actions and words that he puts others into consideration. How a person treats others, friends and family members also matter in determining how good or terrible a person will make as a partner. Most people are not observant enough to pay attention to this, but it is very important if you are serious about knowing who really a person is. This very important aspect will help you a lot in this observation, it portrays that real person. You may not really have been close with him, and he might be hiding some of his characters those few times you both meet. This unconscious attitude of how a person treats others shows what a person is inside and in his heart. Often it has been observed that the way your partner treats his family members, friends, acquaintances, colleagues, in fact anybody he comes in contact with, is actually the way he will treat you. For the moment he may be treating you differently, soon he will likely show you the real him. This is why you should be very observant to watch

YES, ONLY TO THE RIGHT PERSON

out for this attitude in this person. He always shows empathy to people's feelings, wanting to be of help to others at any given moment it calls for? What about him treating others respectfully? Have you seen him allow others to go first before him? This is exactly what he is at heart and not that camouflage he puts up when you are with him; it shows he is kind at heart and not selfish.

These unconscious actions show a lot about a person, and portray his heart condition at any given moment. Take for instance you are driving with him and suddenly you come across an accident scene, very horrific. He stops the car, if possible feels pity or puts effort to render help to those victims. What a wonderful heart he has, always ready to help others; and you too will benefit from this compassionate feeling. You are watching a television with him and it happens that something terrible happens maybe as a result of someone's mistake. Does he show pity first, then pointing out what would have best been done by the victims to avoid such problem? If he does, then he is a person that will always put himself in someone's shoes when passing judgment or giving correction. These are some of the things you really need to take notice, and do not take them for granted. There are so many other ways one can show really that he feels for others, these you will continue to observe in his dealings with other people. One can always put up deceitful actions especially when he is knowledgeable or experienced in life in dealing with a partner. When someone is with people who are less related to him, he displays more of his real qualities, which he does unconsciously. Consciously he might not treat you initially the same way, due to a partial fear of losing you. For some time, he will try as much as possible to suppress this real self, but soon they must manifest. Again how someone behaves when with people in public is very important, that is exactly the way such person will likely behave when in private or with you. This is why lots of people will keep regretting after marriage, because they never paid attention to these eye-openers. They will tell you that this person is not really like this when they started, that he has changed a great deal. Truth is that he didn't change, just that he was not closely observed; especially how he treats others.

If you are finding it difficult trying to deduce this person's real self and the ones he puts up just to please you, this is the time to pay serious attention to his dealings with others. Does he shout at others, or loses his tempter too quickly when with others who are not his loved ones? He may not have shouted at you for the first time, but watch out very soon, he will begin shouting at you. This might be his real self and not that deceit he tricks you to believe. As stated in the introduction of this section, people tend to be more of actors than real, and this should make you to dig deeper to be able to see this person in reality than in the theatre. Come to think of it, in this world of abundant knowledge, one might be reading very well and tries to get polished especially when with people he knows very well or people that know him very well. When this becomes the case, you tend to find it very difficult to see his real self. If this becomes the issue, just take your time to observe how he treats others he meets by accident, especially people he barely knows. Observe how he treats people who he meets by sudden with no connection. This treating of strangers is like seeing how good or bad he is in at heart. This is a fact, one may be good or be compelled to be good to people that have been good to him. One might be under obligation and forced to behave well to people he knows. But the same will not be said of people he barely knows. If he considers others like strangers and treats them with such respect and compassion, then how much more love he will show people he knows. If a person calls you darling and always refers to orders when provoked as idiots, be ready to be called that same idiot when you provoke him, soon.

If someone could be so cold to people's plight, this person may have a cold heart and such heart will surely manifest in his relationship very soon. This, you might not come to terms with until at a certain point in time, then it will gradually manifest, maybe after commitment has been made. Be at alert when you see a partner treating others with

YES, ONLY TO THE RIGHT PERSON

cold feelings, not minding their plight. At a particular point in the relationship he will begin to exhibit this real personality of his. So a better telescopic way to observe this person is when he is in public, how he treats others. This will give you a better picture of this person's heart and intentions toward others which will likely be extended toward you. This same intention he will never fail to bring to bear in the relationship due to the compelling forces of imperfection. Though you should not be quick to rule out that this person is wrong or not, maybe what you need is to lovingly help him see the reason he should change. Like I said, one can easily change his attitude in this regard if that attitude is as a result of influence or upbringing.

It is always good to know the real person you are in a relationship with especially when the relationship will climax to marriage. With this indebt knowledge about his personality you will be able to say yes, you can vow for this person; rather than being disappointed when a commitment has been made. But when a person treats others with severe cruelty and insensitivity, then you may have no other option than to see this person as someone likely to make a wrong partner. Reason is that sooner or later, you will be the next victim when his guards will be let loose. I have this friend, who was contemplating starting a relationship with a particular lady. This man gushed about how wonderful that lady was and how she treated him like a king. Then after I spent times with this couple, I told my friend that this particular lady was just putting up a façade. That she will soon show him the stuff she was made of, then they might already been married. That was a shock to him and he asked to know why I said so. It happened that those times I spent with them I found that this lady treated people with so much insensitivity and she was so selfish and self-centered. Her 'me-first' attitude was so glaring that others can go to hell, so she could have it. But unfortunately she has been pretending to treat her man like a king; this was because she was on a mission. She desperately wanted to settle down with a man.

So if you are still not very convinced about this person, try judging him the way he treats others he meets especially those ones he barely knows. If someone could treat others with insensitivity, you will be treated in such a way. And that you are not treated in such a way at the moment is no guarantee that he won't treat you the same way soon. Though some in love will try as much as possible to hide away this real self from a partner, but once in a while, imperfection will always bring it out.

Tool 2

How This Person Handles Authority

> *"Nearly all men can stand adversity, but if you want to test a man's character, give him power."*
> - **Abraham Lincoln.**

No reasonable person will go into a relationship just to experiment, although some people go into that for this reason. Every wise and mature person will like to climax his relationship with tying the knot. And in marriage, the issue of authority is always a source of worry, the same in a relationship. This is why you hear partners battling for equality in marriage and in relationship. The cause of this is always one person usurping authority, suppressing the other person. And this usurpation and suppression will always be detrimental to the other person involved. Mishandling of this authority goes a long way subjecting one party to severe mistreatment and degradation. Handling of authority is very important and should not be taken for granted especially in relationship. The reason is that power intoxicates according to Karl Max; and if one allows this authority to get into his head, then the other partner will be a victim. If this be the case, it will be very pertinent to use this as another tool in measuring this particular person so as to see his true colour and what sort of partner he will likely turn out to be in a relationship.

Seeing this authority as something very serious in a relationship will make you weigh your partner with this another wonderful tool. There are several questions you have to ask yourself about this person. "How does he handle authority? Does he monopolize power? Does he push instead of lead? Does he apply force in handling authority?" These are some of the questions that will give you a better insight into the kind of person he will be or turn to be in the near future. And the better way to do this is to search out for areas where he handles authority. Try as much as possible to see the way he handles authority in that field, maybe in his field of endeavor. Everybody handles authority in one way or the other, and this you should look into seriously to ascertain what kind of boss he is or will be. Most times an honest and detailed discussion with someone will give you insight as to how he handles authority in capacities he finds himself. If this person is one that will monopolize authority not trying to let people play a part, he doesn't delegate, then be sure that you will be subjected to a relationship of "one man show." He will always like to call the shots wanting you to do just as he has just said. Forget about the door he opens for you when you are out for a dinner, maybe he watched it in a movie, in real life when the relationship goes on, he might be shouting on you to open his door first even before yours. I say this from experience. I have been in organizations where some heads monopolize all the authority, they don't like to delegate. And the effects; few of those leaders I know, run a family where their wives are just second class citizens, relegated to the background. Do you think you will be happy to be in a relationship with a person that makes you look like a second class citizen, relegating you always to the background? This is not a matter of how he treats you now, but how he will treat you in the future.

What about the issue of pushing instead of leading? Does this person show in that capacity he handles authority, that he pushes others to do things even against their will, instead of leading by example? A sign that he will still do the same when the relationship gets serious.

YES, ONLY TO THE RIGHT PERSON

You will only be at the receiving end carrying out the orders whether you like it or not. And when you expect him to practice what he preaches, you are making a big mistake. In a relationship, it is meant to be just two captains, although one should take the driving seat. But taking the driving seat means that the major part of the responsibility lies with this person, to coordinate and not just to force the other person. Imagine two pilots in a cockpit; one takes the wheel while the other gives his support. These two are working so hard to make sure the plane is flown and landed safely. Assuming the one on the driving seat leaves the seat and commands the other to take the steering while he sits beside him drinking. This partner will make a wonderful person only if he leads taking you by hand side by side just as those pilots sit side by side in the cockpit. Observing this partner in this regard will make you come to term with what kind of person he will turn out to be in the area of handling authority, which is very important.

Applying force or being authoritative is another thing to look out for when observing how this partner handles authority. Information that should be humbly disseminated, does he spew them out, making the other person look less important? Is he the kind of person that does not take the feelings of the other person into consideration when forcing this order down the person's throat? Remember you are not in a barrack where words are shouted; even advice comes in form of command. This is a relationship where pleasant words should always come in a soft tone. If a partner deems it fit to always shout at his subjects when dishing out instructions, it becomes a bad sign. He might not have treated you the same way, but he will one day treat you that same way. You will always get hurt, and that is one bad aspect you should not tolerate in a relationship. When in a relationship, words should be spoken softly even if it is a warning; that shows love. One who speaks in force, forces others under his watch to obey orders, and leads with force, is likely going to apply the same method on you very soon. Don't think that those phone calls where he speaks with subjects, constantly shouting the roof down is for nothing, you will be the next victim.

Aside these, what about when he greedily hungers for authority in order to control others? You see the desperation in him to want to have this authority. Some people naturally hunger for power and when you have such person as a partner, you are in for a mistreatment. The person will not stop until he takes the little authority that is due to you, making you come to plead with him as the boss. It goes a long way to portray one as a potential threat to a relationship, although you might not have been affected by this attitude. Imagine when your partner will like to control both your finances and other authorities left for you to handle in a relationship. You dare not do anything; he takes any decision in your absence without informing you and forbids you from taking decision in his own absence. The moment you try doing anything without putting up a formal and official request, he goes at you; getting lots of bashing and all of them. This will again boil down to demoting you to just a second class citizen, instead of a partner. This wrong person is in essence telling you: "stay away, you have nothing good to offer."

When you look at these issues raised concerning the handling of authority, you will come to term that it matters a lot to know how a partner handles authority. It really will affect the relationship especially if the relationship will climax to commitment. This commitment let us say could be marriage; then you will get to understand that your partner mismanages authority which will in essence affect you. Then it will be too late for you to go back. You might be wondering how on earth you didn't see this writing on the wall. You may have seen it, but you may as well didn't think that it mattered. In a relationship, no one should make the other person look unimportant, and no one should assume a bossy attitude toward the other person. It should be made to be a level playing ground where there should be mutual agreement between the partners. Though one person should take the driving seat, and the other

YES, ONLY TO THE RIGHT PERSON

person should respect that. But that does not mean that the person taking the driving seat should use that authority to the detriment of the other person. Observing this person from this perspective of how he presently handles authority in his field of endeavor gives you more details about the person and how he will bring the authority to bear in the relationship. If his subjects are treated like mere subjects you will soon be treated the same way.

Tool 3

The Person's Goals

"If you go to work on your goals, your goals will go to work on you. If you go to work on your plan, your plan will go to work on you. Whatever good things we build end up building us." - **Jim Rohn.**

Human beings describe in other words, are as good or bad as their goals. And like the quotation above, any goal one builds, ends up building the person. These goals go a long way saying the person's aim or his destination. They also tell you what this person has in heart, what this person wants to be and what this person wants to achieve. Again knowing about his goals will also make you to juxtapose them with yours and see if they are in tandem with what really you are working toward too. Goals playing an important role in someone's life will as well be used as a tool to weigh a person. Another better way to read a person's heart is by his goals which will soon become words and actions and as well, shape him. Some people are really good in secrets but not when they bring out their goals or tell them. With someone's goals you can actually tell of a person that will be greedy, insensitive, deceitful, lazy, wicked and so on and so forth. The same goal will also give you insight what hope lies ahead of this person, shaping his thinking. The truth remains that you should have

YES, ONLY TO THE RIGHT PERSON

someone who shares a similar goal with you to be able to make a perfect match.

While a right person is busy making goals that are lasting and beneficial, wrong person is equally busy making goals that are short-lived and selfish. And these goals will always turn to decisions and work plan. Why not take your time, if you think that you really don't know this person well enough to commit yourself; and analyze his goal in life. Does he chase after the wind, things that are practically impossible? This might give you clue as to how confused he might make as a partner going only after vain things. His goals, are they just selfish, satisfying only his interest, and no other person benefiting? Then you might be in with a selfish person pretending to be selfless. Does this person have a goal that will portray him as one who doesn't put family first? Be ready to have a partner who has no word like 'family' in his dictionary, even if he will have, that will be very much later in life. These are some of the things his goals will be saying about him, which you likely might not be seeing at the moment. This is the time to analyze all these things and come to conclusion what really this person is at heart. Look at it this way, in the area of work, does this person set goals on work that will always take into consideration money and not family? If that be the case, then you have met a lover of money, who is ready to compromise, and jeopardize relationships and more important things when money is involved. In the area of acquiring knowledge, does he set goals that will make him judge people and measure things only by their educational status? Such a person is as good as saying that natural wisdom should be thrown away. In fact you can even tell when a person is ready to make a commitment in relationship by his goals in life. There is no better way to understand a partner more than looking at his goals in life and their time frame.

Let us look deeper at the area of goals pertaining work, if one does not bother whether a partner should be neglected emotionally and physically when setting goals related to job, then have it in mind that you will keep begging this person for attention when the relationship goes on. His goals related to work, go a long way to expose his real self as regard work and relationship. Tell me what will prevent this person from leaving you when the offer of getting jobs that will make you both far from each other, comes up? What words and actions cannot tell, goals can tell even going further to explain them. So many times you get to see and hear partners that choose jobs that will make them almost impossible to be together when necessary; already this person has said this by his goals. One of them don't value relationship as much as he values wealth and prestige. In this case, one person continues to suffer in silence while the other person pays no attention as to what the other person goes through. When someone makes a goal that seems not to take into consideration of people he loves, then is as good as saying that those people do not matter. And this could as well throw more light into who this person really might turn out to be in the future. If you don't see it that way, you will regret it later with this person.

What about in the area of setting goals that take into consideration financial gains lone and no other matter? Will you not be convinced that he loves money more than any other thing? Such a person might though love you to an extent, but the love he has for money may be greater than that which he has for you. You really have to pay attention to the kind of goals this person sets, because they say more of him than he would have hidden from you, which you really might not notice. The more you get to know more about his goals, the more you will get to see that hidden him which will only manifest after the relationship must have climaxed maybe to a commitment. Getting to know about this person's goals will help you to match them with yours and see if both will actually be compatible. Take for instance, one makes a goal that will make him bother not about having kids, and you want kids. What a clash it will cause between you and him, making both of you to be at loggerheads all the time.

YES, ONLY TO THE RIGHT PERSON

Most times, people try to get into relationship and want commitment as quickly as possible, how else will you know if this person is ready to get serious other than looking at the goals he sets? Like his future plans, and his goals on the purchase of some certain things in life, these are some of the things that will give you a slight knowledge of what he will not show or tell you. Take for instance, a man that wants to settle down or go into serious relationship with a view to marry will start doing things that will tell you; sooner or later that he will start a family. Yes his goals will say it all. If you are in a relationship and this person seems to find it hard to make a commitment or take the relationship to another level, you can decipher from his goal when likely he will settle down, if only he will. In that regard, you really will know what kind of person you are wasting your time with. The same goes with many other goals, pointing out what really this person is, and not just what he makes you to believe he is.

I have this very close friend whom I have known for long. Though he seemed to be a good man, but there is more of him I got to know when I started analyzing his goals. To my surprise, I found out that this friend though appeared so good and nice, had a dubious mind. How did I get to know this? I looked at his goals concerning wealth; I found out that he always liked to cut corners and compromise. Though he had not exhibited such toward me, but I didn't really need a soothsayer again to tell me to be very careful with this friend on issues related to money. These goals can as well be seen as work plan and tools one works with. And looking at a person with gun as his tool will tell you that such a person shoots. Though upbringing and situation vary, and these tend to affect the goals people set in life. But at the end, these goals will reflect what a person is inside, in the heart or will like to be in the near future. Even if it has not been manifested in the person's life, the goals will soon build him into what he plans. Tactfully asking this person what his goals are, both for long and short term, and observing him pursue them, will as well make you have insight into what he really prioritize in his life. Just as a biblical verse, "by their fruits you shall know them." By his goals too, you shall know him more.

Tool 4

The Person's Friends

"You can't tell me more than I can tell myself when I see your friends." - **O.D. Chimex.**

And this comes in line with a Mexican proverb: "Tell me who your friends are and I will tell you who you are." This axiom never changes no matter the test of time. Some will go a long way to tell you that they can be friends with just anybody and still, will not act one bit like that person. A first look at this statement, one will be forced to believe it is true, but a critical assessment of the statement placing it side by side with real life experiences will prove the statement to be mendacious. The friends one makes tell more of whom the person really is or will likely be soonest, despite the camouflage. One who doesn't like violence will find it difficult to associate with someone that is violent. And one who hates stealing will as well find it very difficult to come closer to a known thief not to talk of being friends with him. It is obvious that when someone fools himself to think that he can actually make friends with people of characters he hates, then it is also obvious that the person has gradually begun to lower his standard and stand, taking in those nasty characters of those friends gradually. And this will continue to have subtle effect on the person till he begins to see reason to justify such a friend's actions thereby seeing it as normal thing to do. It will only be birds of a feather that will always flock together. For this reason it becomes important to tell what really a person is or will be, using his friends to weigh him. Friendship becomes another tool, giving you insight into a person's desires and choices.

You need to seriously look at this person's friends to be able to come to in-depth knowledge of who he is. It is not just enough to take a person by his words or few displays. It will be enough when you have at your fingertips what will likely not be said or acted. It is obvious that some people don't really know the person they are about to start or in a relationship with. This person goes a long way to play hide and seek, making hidden his true self. What do I mean by this? Assuming this person does a dirty thing far away from where you could lay your hands on or see it. Do you think you can imagine in this whole wide world what this person does behind your back? There is no way you can lay your hands on what he does behind you if not look at the friends that comes around him. Some are very good at covering their tracks very well, at least for a longer time. When you get into a relationship with such person, you will find it difficult to get to know this person in the behind. But a closer watch on the friends he keeps, whether on social media or real life, will give you a clue what kind of person he is or will become. These friends tell you what kind of business he might be doing at your back and which one he intends going into sooner. Don't you think that a person who keeps gamblers as friends might either be engaging in gambling or contemplating gambling?

The other day I was reading a local newspaper and a man was arrested in a country for kidnapping. This man fessed up that he had a wife and children living in different country, while he did his sordid business in another country. Then when asked what business his wife knew him for. He said that he told his wife he was dealing in clothes and foot wears. What a poor naïve woman, when she comes to term with this shocking revelation that her husband does such illegal business and has been arrested. I am sure that the woman was just ignorant to take into consideration her husband's friends, the few times he stayed with them. There must be few of his accomplices visiting his house anytime he comes into town; or sometimes, he must be hanging out with them. But she was so ignorant to get to know this and take this into consideration. She took the man by just his words and neglected to observe him by the friendship he made. This is why you have to pay attention, judge and weigh a partner by his friends; there must be signs to show that his friends are what he is. Like poles, will always attract like poles; and birds of a feather will always flock together. Those few friends that you know that he entertains will likely be acting like him. So watch them, watch their characters any time you come across them, you must see your partner in them. These people, for the fact that they have nothing to do with you, and owe you no apology for their actions; that will make them be their real selves always when you are around them.

He keeps friends that are flirts, and you think he won't be a flirt? Let us assume that he is not, but there is more chances that soon he will be thought to flirt just like his friends. Even if he doesn't flirt, his standards and stand on flirting will continue to diminish. And before you know it, you will become a victim to this bad attitude. This is because when with his friends, their conversations will likely be centered on their personal lives, and when the lives of such friends are bad, they will always feed him with bad stories and experiences of theirs. When these stories and bad personal experiences keep recording in his memory, you will be at the receiving end bearing the brunt. Friends a person keeps matter a lot if you don't know. Not just kids or adolescents are influenced by peer pressure, adults, even aged ones too, are influenced by peer pressures. So why not search out by looking at the friends he keeps to see what kind of person he is or will likely be. Rate him by his friends and see his kind of friends as his real self. Remember you are keen about getting to know this person very well and deeply, this tool will help you as well to know him better.

This should not be taken for granted, your life is at stake and your emotions and heart too are on the line. There will not be anything like; he is different from his friends, unless those people are not friends that he spends time with. Assuming a person doesn't smoke cigarette, but he stays so often and close with someone who smokes, when such one smokes. Tell me how such person won't be inhaling the fume; and if he does; how he won't suffer smoke-related diseases like the other person. So his friends really have a role to play in his life and it affects you. Every precious stone dug out, took earnest and dogged effort.

There is no way you could just see raw diamond lying on the surface of the earth. You must spend time, resources and other opportunity cost to be able to dig out this precious stone; the same with getting into a real relationship with the right person. It does not come on a platter of gold; effort must be put on your side to know someone before you make commitment. This is not luck, and don't be too quick to throw away your heart and emotion to someone who will rubbish them at the end. It is foolishness to dissipate your time trying to get a very wrong thing right. That effort should best be put in searching out for the right person instead of wasting it with the wrong person.

Friends will always tell you about someone who you really might find difficult to know. If this be the case, take your time to observe this person's friends thoroughly to see what you are not likely seeing. The effort is worth it to search out for this right person. The more you see this person keeping very wrong persons as friends, who you yourself will find difficult to associate with, the more wrong he will likely be as a partner. This should as well make you to see him the same way you see these wrong friends of his. Though a good person might likely influence someone bad for good, but only when such a bad person has made up his mind to be good. But in most cases, the bad one turns around to influence a good one wrongly. If a single person has more of friends that are married, then soon he might follow the path of his friends. And if he has more of friends that are single, even though he is

YES, ONLY TO THE RIGHT PERSON

married, soon he will behave single. There is no way you can totally disassociate one from his friends, they must always have a positive correlation.

Tool 5

What This Person Always Talks About

"Speech is the mirror of the soul; as a man speaks, so he is." - **Publilius Syrus.**

Sometimes you hear people joke, say things in a funny way to make others laugh. Some will go on and on making jokes with a particular thing more often, that you begin to understand that his whole thought is centered on that particular thing. Do you think the person is just being humorous? Though he might be, but that is equally telling a whole lot about the person he is without him knowing actually. In real life, we unconsciously tell others the kind of person we are by the words we say and the way we say it. And this goes with a bible verse that says: "Out of the abundance of the heart the mouth speaks." You can't say what you don't have in your heart, and what you have in your heart contributes a lot to who you are. Most of the Secret Services and Intelligences work with this, nailing people with their words. Psychologist and Psychiatrists also use this to tell more of a person at a particular point in time when some behaviours are being examined. If these aficionados and experts could see words spoken as relevant in understanding human behaviours and characters, then why not you, also apply it in searching out if a person will be a right person. This is

YES, ONLY TO THE RIGHT PERSON

another wonderful tool that could give you more insight into the real personality of a person.

Though a particular situation might make one to begin to say something continuously at a moment; that also will tell you what this very person has turned into or about to turn into at that point in time. It might be that such words have taken over the person's thought, which will engender him acting like the words he says. If a person talks about a particular thing with enthusiasm, then he will also do or act that way sooner or later. It might also be that that is what he acts always. Before one does anything, he must have uttered it several times or things similar to that prior to acting it. And if you being in a relationship with a person pay attention to his words, you will learn a great deal about the person. Something happens about another person, observe and listen to this partner react to that issue with words. "If it happened I were the one, I will never let go, head must roll, an eye for an eye." Maybe you think this was said out of deep sympathy for the victim. Then a similar thing happens another different time, he repeated words similar to what he said the other time, telling how he will go on revenge mission. You continue to observe him speak about revenge always when things happen to others. Yet you don't know that this person might be vindictive. He has not shown you that, but he might be showing it to others behind you. If he revenges others, what will make him not to revenge you, though not in a visible way, but in a more subtle way? Listen to what he talks always, that is what his mind thinks always and his actions will go toward that direction. We can never separate our actions from our words, it is almost impossible. Whatever one talks always must be what his personality is in the real sense.

He talks about sex always, coining every matter to sex-related jokes, and you think he doesn't like what he talks always? He might not be a sex addict yet; but most people who are sex addicts always say it out in words. This could give you insight what a person might likely be in the near future. Someone's choice of words goes further to tell you about his moral standard and the level of discipline this one has. And if one shows by his words that he is such a loose person without moral guards, it will likely make a wrong partner in a relationship. He may have thrown morals to the dogs. The same way someone who has no discipline will not bring discipline to bear on any activity he ventures into, this his words will always show. Like earlier said, in the world we live today, people are more of actors and actresses playing just by a script. These people are very good in putting up a fake appearance in order to deceive others and for this reason it becomes wise to put these things into consideration so as to decipher the person he is within. The other day there was an online news about a legend who made some nasty comments, and few hours later, he tendered an unreserved apology for such comments, that those comments weren't really who he was inside. A wise person will laughed it off as just hogwash to deceive gullible ones, and that was it, though some people will believe him by his words. But as he said it, that was exactly how he was at heart, just that he tried his best to put up a pretense. Someone might never have acted what he says, but believe it one day he will act it.

It is not just a joke if that particular subject alone interests him all the time. How could you be so naïve and ignorant not to take into consideration his words? You think they don't really matter? They do matter a lot. People who tend to be very violent always say words that depict violence most of the time. When there is a particular issue, instead of them to say things that will show they want dialogue, the first thing they will say will be in line with eye for eye, notion. Even words will tell you also more of a person's upbringing and where he is coming from no matter how hard he tries to hide it. This is very true with people who come from the ghetto; there words will always be a mark of identity. They seem to be very conversant with slang, and this they go further to speak always. Someone's lifestyle as well reflects on his words, even the past life style too, he exhumes them by his words. Have you wondered why people keep using vulgar language? This is because they either fancy the lifestyle associated with such vulgar language or that they are really living such lifestyle at the moment. In as much as you want to know this person better, you have to pay serious attention to his words always. This reminds me of what I used to do when I was a kid. If I commit a vice, let us say I spoiled something and ran away without being noticed. When that is uncovered and an older person tells such to me, the questions I will be asking will really tell you that I might be guilty. "Did they say I was the one that spoils it?" Questions like this I will be asking. At first remembering this, I was tempted to look at it as childish acts, but they are not, adults do same as well. There is no way you can escape from saying what your heart has in abundance at one time or the other. So keep this yet another tool in your possession to be able to use it in understanding this partner more than those few acts will put up.

The law court as well always uses this tool very well during proceedings. Keep someone in the dock and bombard him with questions upon questions, he will succumb to telling what really happened, no matter how a pathological liar he is. Words said, are very important tool to give you insight into what a person is or will likely be in the future. "Sorry it is a slip of tongue. I am just joking, I didn't mean it." Don't believe it, there must be a link between what he says and what he is. Sometimes people who are smart enough will give someone alcohol to make him let his guards down when talking. And in such situation, deep secrets are always revealed unconsciously. This does not mean you have to sit your partner down and harass him with questions to know his heart; some might give you well-polished deceitful words if you do it that way. The emphasis is on words spoken unconsciously most of the time when no question is asked.

There are other various ways to see what a person is by his words, and what his actions will become in such a situation. Constant conversation with this person will begin to reveal more of who the person is by his words. And this calls for spending time with this person constantly in a very formal setting so as to have meaningful conversations that will be revealing. Though actions speak louder than words, but words say more of what the actions will be. Words speak even more of what will take years to be turned into action, in this regard words act like a prophet. In as much as you pay attention to actions, pay attention too to words says all the time and the way it is being said, with the attendant gestures. These attendant gestures are very important when one speaks. People who beat their partners have often made verbal signals and they were ignored by the victim. If someone tells you something and demonstrates it with the exact gestures, don't you think the person must have practiced that or that he has vivid picture of it in his mind? Take a person's words the same way you will take the person, if those words become a constant occurrence.

Tool 6

The Person's Scale of Preference

"Desires dictate our priorities, priorities shape our choices, and choices determine our actions." - **Dallin H. Oaks.**

We have talked about some of the tools that will tell you more of a person you want to make a commitment with; and the list continues. Coming to how this person prioritizes things is another way to getting to know what kind of person one really is. Everybody has lots of things to do and achieve, and no doubt, you have a slight attachment to all you do because your survival and wellbeing depend on them. But the importance one places on those life activities does not just stop at its usefulness to the person's existence, it goes beyond that. It goes a long way to tell so much about a person that you never could understand ordinarily. The same way the types of friends one keeps, his goals, words could tell more of the person, priorities can as well give you a deeper insight of the kind of person this one is. Looking at these statements at first, one might begin to wonder how this could be possible, and I tell you that it is very possible to get to know who a person is by the way he prioritizes his activities. The funny part of it is that though this prioritization is a conscious effort, it as well consciously says more about who a person is or will be in the near future. You will also apply this superb tool in examining a person you are in a relationship with, thoroughly.

In Economics, we are told that every rational being must have a scale of preference. This scale of preference simply put is the detailed listing of a person's needs, prioritizing them according to their order of importance at that moment. If this be the case, scale of preference should always be part and parcel of one's life. And wealth has to play two major roles in this scale of preference. It is part of the scale of preference and as well influences this scale of preference just like other factors. This is so, because we have insatiable wants that will continue to increase and vary almost all the time. If wealth exerts great influence in determining the scale of preference then we will use it to analyze this scale of preference. The same way wealth exerts a great influence on someone's life, knowingly or unknowingly, it imparts on a person's priorities as well. There are other factors that should also influence this scale of preference, this the right person also takes into consideration.

Look at this person's scale of preferences how he prioritizes them, and if wealth is placed at the topmost of someone's scale of preference, then there must be trouble and it tells more of a person than you could see. It tells you what the person values more, and what he will give the first attention before any other thing. A good person might automatically change to be bad tomorrow just because of wealth; the same way a bad person might turn to be good because of wealth too. In some countries, some will tell you that a hungry man is an angry man. The other time I was listening to some skits and the clown said that the level of wealth one has could determine the level of humility or arrogance the person could have. And that is true somehow especially if such one places so much emphasis on wealth. More of the reason tramps are so humble, and some rich people are arrogant. This person is in essence saying that the way a person places wealth above all other priorities could say a whole lot about the person and determines what sort of person he might be.

YES, ONLY TO THE RIGHT PERSON

What else could be understood about a person in the way he places wealth first in his scale of preference, you might ask? If this person pushes wealth to be the first in his scale of preference in life, then you might likely be with person that will soon dump you for that wealth. You are surprised right? But don't be; this placement tells you deeper things about him. The truth is that in life, there are other things that should come first and top in our scale of preference. Imagine this partner that has wealth as the first in his scale of preference, how he will react when matter of wealth and life is at stake. Throw a box filled with money in the river and throw his partner into that same river and ask him to save them one after another. Off toward the money box this person will proceed first; and after he must have gotten the money box, then he will come for his partner. One who ranks wealth as the first in life is always a wrong person to be with. You might find it confusing to believe, but it is always the hard truth. And most people still turn a deaf ear to this, yet in the long run they will be the ones to cry.

This same person, having wealth at the top of his scale of preference does not really mean that he will write down a list and give money number one position before you could decipher this. By his actions, he will continue to tell what positions wealth is in his life. Imagine he keeps skipping important things related to family, relationship, or life, just because of avoidable money matters. The same way he might run away from his wedding day just because of a business call he get. I saw a meme the other day on the internet and I couldn't stop laughing at it. A man was on the floor in front of the church pulpit with a preacher having his bible stood still by his side. This man on the floor was sitting, and his phone clenched on his left ear, making a call. It happened that this man was meant to be receiving deliverance from the pastor; and his phone rang, he jumped up like a stag to receive that business call. Imagine the disappointment in the eyes of the pastor; probably this man must be from the underworld. Similar things happen in real life, where people always abandon more important things just for wealth related issues which could as well be postponed.

People that place money at a very high priority always love money more than anything and this goes a long way to tell more about them, how they will treat others when the issue of money is involved. It does not mean that the person might be poor or rich before he shows this great attachment to wealth. Anybody could be that kind that loves wealth so much whether rich or poor. Someone who attaches this great and unwholesome importance to wealth is influenced by wealth at a very great extent. This is why you see someone who is an average income earner, when he makes more wealth, changes to something different; so arrogant and audacious. It is not really the wealth that changed him; that personality is in him just that this wealth helped to bring it out. And he must have been exhibiting such trait, that he will likely be so when wealth comes.

I have also come to understand from experiences that people who attach so much importance to wealth than usual are always stingy, they are scrooge. This is because they will always find it hard to let that wealth go. And stinginess is really a sign of a person likely not going to make a good partner in a relationship. Imagine when you have to wear a set of clothes for long and eat the same kind of food often, simply because this person doesn't want to let this money be spent. Yes he thinks that every other things matter not more than wealth, therefore, wealth should be cherished and the other things neglected. Don't take it lightly when a partner places so much importance on things that should not be, it might be how the person sees those things, and that is him, from inside. If money commands great influence in this person's life, don't be surprise that if you come in between him and this wealth, you will be a victim.

Not just money, the same goes with what other things someone places first in his life, shows you what kind of person he might be. Take

YES, ONLY TO THE RIGHT PERSON

again for instance one that places family at very low position in his scale of preference, such a person will likely not make a good one to start a family with. If one is always fond of placing unimportant things above important things, then it tells how childish and selfish such one is. And talking about other things that influence this person's scale of preference is also very important. Although money exerts great influence on someone's scale of preference; but it should not always be money all the time for a wise person. Emotions and passion and other things could as well influence someone's priority, even other people's feelings could influence someone's scale of preference. And only a right person will not want money to have that overwhelming influence in influencing his scale of preference. Take your time to observe this person what he values most especially when the issue of making a choice out of choices comes out. That will tell you more about a person, than you will be told or meant to understand.

Tool 7

The Person's Hobby

"The only thing I can tell you about myself is the only thing that my hobbies will tell you about me."
- O.D. Chimex.

Life could be so boring if one has no hobby to enjoy at his convenient time. No matter how hardworking a person is, he must have time to do things that he loves doing. Those things that he loves doing could tell you more of this person that you should know, which his attitude and other camouflage are making difficult to see. Hobbies are those things that you like doing right? Yes they are, and not just those things that you do regularly for pleasure. That you enjoy doing something, though you have not done it for once, makes it a hobby. Like myself, I like watching football, though it has been decades I kicked a ball. But that does not mean that I will not kick a ball again, sooner or later I will. In fact if opportunity presents itself this moment, with a football right in front of me, I will not hesitate to kick it very well. Again, I loved watching wrestling, even though I didn't fight. But I think that if that temptation to fight came my way then, I would have found it difficult to resist applying those skills I watched in the wrestling. Have you wondered why some people choose some professions? Mostly it is because they are their hobbies and their way of

YES, ONLY TO THE RIGHT PERSON

life, they love doing them and developed an attraction for those professions. A person who hates violence will never in his life join the military. The same way a person who watches violence will one day practice that violence, unknowingly, because it exerts a great influence on the person's mind.

Hobby does two things in a person; it shows what a person is inside, and as well, shapes who a person is. Since your aim is to know the secret person of the heart, of this partner you want to entrust your heart to, then you have to take this into consideration is trying to search out his real personality. Have you wondered why people always attach the role an actor or actress plays in a movie to their real life? Imagine when one constantly plays a role of an arrogant person in movies, and he does it best and enjoys playing such roles in movies. The conclusion will be that this person has a connection with this role in his life; that might be near the truth. Most times, someone who has a total different nature will never fit into a role that is the direct opposite of what he is. See it that way with the hobby one enjoys, irrespective of whether this person has really done it or he just watches it. He might not really want to show you the more of him, but now his hobbies are telling you that which was hidden. Nature is so funny sometimes, our personalities reflect on what we like and don't like. This reminds me of a particular friend, when we were in secondary school. He liked violent games always and played them always too. This particular boy always found it very easy to engage in fight, very difficult for him to resists the temptation of fighting when it presented itself. And this became his way of life all through the days we were in school. Bring him to love games that have to do with working the brain to achieve a result, he will run away from those. This boy was one of the dumbest fellows we had then in our class. His hobbies then defined him, making him to fit in just into violent acts.

The same with someone who likes indoor games, mostly such a person is always an introvert, finding it hard to socialize; just like someone that loves outdoor games, mostly extrovert. Someone's personality will always tally with what he likes doing all the time, and not just what he does all the time. This fact you should have in mind when you try to search out for this person's real self. The more you get to know this person's hobbies, the more you will begin to understand that he really loves doing, even though he may not have been doing them. Give him opportunity to do so, he will not hesitate to. Hobbies are not forced, they are innate in everybody, and as personalities vary, hobbies vary too. But this does not really mean that people don't learn things new; they do. But the fact is that when one enjoys kind of hobbies that are just strange or not really loved by so many, you should be at alert maybe that must be what really the person is inwardly. No matter how a person tries to learn new thing, if that innate love in him is not there, he won't enjoy doing that always. In fact it is only when a person has innate love for something, even though he might not know how to do it, that he will go learn how to do it.

This is why military and other Special Forces trained for killing, are always taken to a practice ground, to always practice shooting. They do this, not only to make them perfect shooting, but to also make those trainees love shooting all the time. And one cannot love shooting if he doesn't have an atom of violence in him. The same goes with many other hobbies that people love doing, they really will tell you what manner of person he is or will be. Take for instance one who has a penchant for gambling, this person loves doing it, not just because he needs money, it is because he enjoys doing it. This goes a long way to say more about the person than what you might really not have known very well. This tool will help you to come to understand what really his interest is on, what he enjoys doing most of the time. Now take a look at those people that always enjoy watching romantic movies, most of them either are very romantic or they will like to get romantically involved with someone soon. Likewise those whose hobby is money making, they are always ready to do anything to make money. So this

YES, ONLY TO THE RIGHT PERSON

list continues on and on to tell more of a person, even if the person does not do that at the moment, he will do it in the future.

Think about this, when you want to be successful in life, will your hobby not be to read motivational books and interviews of great people? Definitely it will, because you want to be just like them. If you are not bothered about being very successful, you will never like reading motivational books and interviews. I once had a colleague whose hobby was watching pornographic materials. His cell phone had all sorts of sordid materials ranging from girlie pictures to hardcore movies. Then what was his life style? It was just exactly those things he loved watching. Those things went a great deal in shaping his lifestyle as well building him into a sex addict. So when one is always excited doing a particular thing or revels in it when others do it, that might really be his lifestyle, though circumstances may restrict him not to practice such at that moment. If one is such a materialistic person, you won't find it surprise to see the person loving things that portray excessive materialism. And if one doesn't like driving a car, he will find it hard saving to buy a car. It does not always mean that a person will exactly be like what he likes doing. Here is just making it clear that what one likes, say a whole lot about who he is and what he will likely be.

So taking your time out for this real search is not just easy but the effort is what it and you will be happy you did so. Some will always say that a broken relationship is better than a broken marriage, and I agree with that. Don't be fooled by a false pretense. It is better to get to know this person very well and then decide if you will cope with such person, than being inundated by surprises after commitment has been made. Let your relationship not be a gift box that when you open it, you take whatever you see in it. Let it be an open gift that you may decide to take or not, judging by the content. Though environment and upbringing also contribute a lot to what someone may take as hobby, but the truth remains that when a person does what he likes; he does it with enthusiasm and passion. And what a person does with interest and joy, always tells who he is inside.

Tool 8

The Person's Job

"Everyone has been made for some particular work, and the desire for that work has been put in every heart." -
Rumi.

Talking about job, how it affects a person and the impact it will have on a person, telling you a whole lot about the person cannot be underestimated. It has a great influence; in fact it is two sided. There is no way you will totally separate the kind of job one does from the kind of person such one is. Telling more about a person by the kind of job he does boils down to how this person sees any job or any means of livelihood and what kind of job he does. Looking at a person from these two angles will help you to have more insight into what kind of person one is and will be. In some parts of the world, people tend to work so hard while in other parts, people are exposed to not just working hard, but also working smartly. There is also a tendency that these working hard and smartly will always affect the kind of life one lives, directly and indirectly. Again sadly, in some parts of the world, people also are exposed to be lazy, cutting corners to succeed. Don't you think that these kinds of mindset as a result of the views on jobs will affect those people individually? Definitely it will, to a great extent, and this will undoubtedly affect what kind of person one becomes in a relationship. Apart from being affected by these external factors, what about in a situation where one has been taught to work hard and as well shown how to work hard in a legitimate way. Then such a person chooses a job and his own way of working that job, will that not tell you something about such a person? Observation of a person using his job as a yardstick will tell you deeper things about a person.

Look at situation where one is lazy, cuts corners at work and does not like working hard; will it not tell you more of what a person is or will be in the near future? Of course this will tell you a whole lot about someone's personality more than just words would say. Don't you think you will find it very difficult to cope in a relationship with someone that finds it difficult to work hard? Seriously you will find it hard to cope with such a person. This person has been cloned to not put effort to make anything succeed, not at all. The more you work so hard to make the relationship work, the more this lazy person will sit down and watch you do it all by yourself. He cares not, and has no mindset to put effort in anything to make it work. This is why you hear lots of partners complain that they are the only one putting effort to let this relationship work; while the other partner redundantly watches passively. This partner has not shown any other serious danger signs of being a wrong person, but he finds it hard to put effort in anything he engages in because he is lazy. Mostly, some people that are lazy don't learn it; it is in their nature to be lazy. The implication of this may be trickling down to affect virtually all parts of the person's life, even his thinking. No one will like to end up with a partner who will be so lazy to contribute to the wellbeing of the relationship. This is a kind of person that might likely make a bad husband who depends on his wife to cater for the family. Or be that bad wife that leaves the home to be so unkept that and she finds it hard to prepare meal for the family. So a person's attitude to job will give you more insight into the manner of person he is or will be.

YES, ONLY TO THE RIGHT PERSON

A person that is lazy toward job tends to be lazy in everything he does in life, and finds it very hard to support even emotionally in a relationship. I mean, how will you expect him to provide emotional support to you when you need it, when he is lazy, and does no work? Get him a very juicy job; he will lazily throw it away; the same way he will continue giving excuses as to his reasons for being lazily involved in the relationship. I had a friend who complained bitterly about his father's aloofness in the family. I asked him what attitude his father had at his job. I was surprised to hear he doesn't keep a job; and that he had worked lots of jobs but gave flimsy excuses to quit those jobs. From his lamentations, I found out that his father saw it as a task to render his obligation as the head of the house as well, the same way he took those jobs. And when it came to getting advice from him as a father, he found it hard to think out advice to give his family. This goes a long a way to tell you that people's attitude to job can be brought to bear on their personality as well. The more one exhibits a lazy attitude to work, the more this shows that the person will likely make a wrong partner. How do you expect him to keep a relationship when he can't keep a job? What about someone that likes cutting corners at jobs when it is evident that that cutting corners is as a result of laziness? Such one will likely be bad as a partner too. This person has in his nature or has made it his nature to cut corners in all he does, the same way he will be cutting corners in your relationship. Issues arise, instead of settling it once and for all; he cuts corners to solve the problem temporary. And do not expect such a person to be straight forward in a relationship.

Then what about the kind of job that someone does? It is indubitable that what a job a person does is him, believe it or not. Someone runs a strip club and you think he might not be a stripper? Someone deals on illicit drugs and you think he might not be a drug addict too? You are really searching deeply to get to know the right person for you, so beam your searchlight to the kind of job he does as well. It will tell you more you need to know about the person. The other day I was talking with an old man in the neighborhood and he was narrating his experiences to me. He mentioned about a lady that ran to him for advice that her husband beats her always. I interrupted him and asked him what kind of job he does? The old man said: "he owns a drinking parlor." And I asked him: "Do you expect him not to be a drunk?" The old man was dumb, looking at me pensively. If this person does drugs, then expect him to always taste this substances and get high most of the times acting on the influence of those substances. If one sells liquor, how then will not expect him to taste the liquor?

Job exposes people too making them do strange things according to the dictates or principles of the job. I was reading some online articles and I found out that some jobs do expose people to doing some funny bad habits. If that be the case, why should start a relationship with someone whose job will likely make him do bad things? Sadly, some families have failed because of this job exposure. Some relationships broke up because of the kind of job a partner does. A person accepting a particular job will go a long way to tell you more of that person or what the person will turn to be in the near future. While searching out to know the real person, make sure you don't put this issue aside; it is important and has an influence on someone. A right thinking person when he does a job that will have negative influence on him wastes no time to call it a quit; because he has seen calamity and proceeds to conceal himself.

Your life is likely at stake if this person does a risky job as well; this is very important. Take for instance a situation where you have to always think whether this person will survive without harm at work; how emotionally debilitating it will be. Think of the guiltiness you will always feel when your partner does job that put other people's life on the line. And think how dangerous you will be when you both hang out in public. My elder brother had a classmate then, who had a soldier as a father. And guess what, this boy whose father was a soldier was trained with brutality due to the harshness of the father in disciplining them.

YES, ONLY TO THE RIGHT PERSON

And guess what again, this same boy subjected some of his classmates to bullying. The same with a particular news of a legendary wrestler who shot himself dead including his wife and kid. Why won't he resort to violence to prove his frustration when violence has been his way of life as a job? What about the work hazards, will it not come to bear on this person's life in the future, maybe cutting his life short? These are some of things that this person's job will let you to know, so as not to be a sudden climber and hasten faller. Observe his job to know things that you might not know at the moment but will come to bear on either you or the relationship in the future. And if a person makes his job in such a way that it looks clandestine, then there is something fishy about the person and his job.

Tool 9

How the Person Handles Resources

"Watch out the way you manage your business, it might be the way you will manage yourself; the way you manage your resources, it might be the way you will manage others." - **O.D. Chimex.**

There are whole lots of things to learn from the way a person manages resources, as relates to a person's personality and mental state. Making use of this to weigh a partner in a relationship is very important. Before going into details to talk about this tool, I will like to narrate a brief experience. In the neighborhood, I knew this young man, who worked so hard. He will do all sorts of menial jobs to survive, and was ready to work from dawn to dusk. Suddenly I stopped seeing him in the neighborhood, for months he disappeared. The next time I set my eyes on him, he looked totally different and he looked like someone who was convalescing. I never cared to ask, till rumor began spreading that he was admitted in a psychiatric hospital all those times he was in oblivion. Though we greeted very well, I never cared to ask him if what I heard was true or not. This same young man after recovering went back to working hard like he had ever done. One year later, he began looking emaciated and famished. People became conscious of his new looks, and his disposition began changing again; he became aggressive, always looking fisticuffs. Then one night around eight o'clock, he ran into our compound shouting as if someone was after him; everybody was afraid. Message was sent across to his family and they came to take him. What prompted the sending of message across to his family members was his strange attitude, the ventriloquize and countenance. His saddened father narrated with pains his ordeals and the mental sickness the young man has been suffering for long. From his story, it happened that anytime those symptoms of insanity returned that the young man will squander all money he made and the ones he saved. Years after, I noticed that those kind of squandering are associated with mental state of the person suffering.

Why did I tell this story? Someone's efficiency in the management of resources most times is based on the person's level of intelligence quotient. It also goes further to tell on how balanced one is mentally and emotionally. Though there are other exogenous factors that might influence this, but one's way of managing resources will tell you what type of a person he is, if you are observant enough to link this management with other characters of the person. What one spends mostly on will as well tell you what kind of person he is and his interest. So with this, you could as well try to know how right or wrong this person will be in a relationship. The more prudent a person is, the more chances that this person really is not just ready for a relationship, but also wise, and mentally and emotionally balanced to handle relationship as well. Some will find it very difficult to believe that the way someone handles and manages resources say more about the person.

Sometimes I read about very wealthy people that went broke as a result of mismanagement of resources, and I tell you, go check these people well, they might have broken relationship too. And if the relationship is not broken, then it must be shaky. If you cannot manage resources, how can you manage a relationship? And how can such person manage his life as well? If resources entrusted into a person's care is not safe, how then could you expect a partner to be safe in his care? This goes with some saying that everything is business, it requires management; and that is very true. Though unforeseen occurrences might befall one to make him mismanage resources, but when such is not the case, then this same person will always mismanage a home as well. This should be a thing to take seriously when considering the rightfulness of a partner in a relationship. In some countries, some are advocating to allow real time resource managers to handle the affairs in the political scene. This notion is based on the confidence and antecedents of these resources managers have in the economic field. If such big time resource managers could over the years be able to manage resources very well, there is possibility that such ones have management skills as well. Funny the same goes with relationship, the way a person handles resources will tell you more of him that you need to know, and the likelihood that he has the ability to handle what is put in his care. Though not all good resource managers will make a good partner, but managing resources well also counts in what kind of person one is. If a person is too extravagant and wastes resources, does it not show lack of maturity on the part of the person? How then do you think you can cope with such one?

You can tell too if a person is mentally mature to make a good partner by the way he handles resources. A rational and mature person knows that these resources are scarce and that his wants are insatiable. So even if he has plenty of wealth, these insatiable wants will soon consume all the resources. Therefore prudence is required on his part with regards to these resources. One who will likely make a right person sees relationship that way, being able to handle the relationship with the same care he employs with regards to resources. He sees you as a scarce resource that should be managed efficiently to avoid allowing insatiable wants to destroy the relationship. Anything he has, he holds it very preciously to avoid losing it. Give him a little resources, he will grow it more; the same way he will grow a relationship to blossom into commitment. He takes things seriously and hates waste; he shows seriousness too in anything he does. But one with characteristics of a wrong person will have a very poor management of resources, thereby wasting relationship the same way he wastes resources. Not serious in relationship, the same way he is not serious in managing resources. So how a person manages resources will tell you more of what you may not really get to know just by looking at his character. The more you keep observing the way he handles resources, the more you begin to peer into his heart to know the kind of person he will likely be.

Being prudent and efficient does not mean being a scrooge or a miser. In fact this goes further to tell you more about a person with such attitude, the likelihood of being a better partner or not. Resources are part and parcel of everyone's life the same way your partner will be if such partner is being taken seriously. In this regard therefore, management of one will indirectly have a bearing on the other. He might likely hoard his time, his emotions and resources as well in the relationship, because it is in him to hoard things. And it tells more of the state of his intelligence quotient. Does it not amount to foolishness when one hoards resources and in the process suffers himself? Does it not amount to stupidity if one hoards what will be due to his partner knowing fully well that it will bring disagreement and possibly a breakup? Unless this person does not value that relationship, and that tells you more about the person or his intention in the relationship.

In as much as you cannot totally judge a person's way of managing resources to have an overbearing influence on a relationship; but then you cannot as well totally take it away from his personality. It definitely has a bearing in one's real self, much more than could be said. Have in mind that we are talking about various ways in which you can get to know this person more than what is obtainable in his behaviours. What he likely spends on will also go a long way to give you a slight knowledge what you need to know about this person. When one does more of spending instead of investing, it might show that this person will only be at the receiving end of the relationship instead of giving. It might also show that this person thinks less of the future, just the present he thinks. And how do you think a person who thinks less of the future will think of taking the relationship to the future? He might not likely picture your relationship in the future. There are other things that the way this person handles resources could tell you about a person with regard to his inner self which is hidden. How good he will be as a wonderful provider as a partner would as well be revealed. And any relationship being taken to the next level should be weighed so as to be sure if you could likely want such a person as a partner. Making these serious observations will make you to come to conclusion as to what you could condone or not in a partner.

Tool 10

The Person's Addiction

"When you smoke the herb, it reveals you to yourself and to others around you." - **Bob Marley.**

As humans, we all have an attachment to something else. There are things that we like to depend on all the time to be able to be happy. No single person is exempted when it comes to having a strong attachment to something else. These things that we are attached to, also make us happy when we are likely not in a good mood. But it becomes a problem when one is so strongly attached to something that you find it hard to separate such a person from that thing, especially if that thing is harmful. The worse being when such addiction is detrimental to one's health or endangers others around him. Your addiction might not really be just on harmful or intoxicating substance like drugs or liquor. It might be that you are almost depending on something else solely that when you don't do such thing, it seems as if some part of you is missing. Is There a particular thing that you will find hard; very hard to stop doing? That is your own addiction, believe it or not. This affects a person's life too, showing who really he is. And this also will always be brought to bear in a relationship with regards to weighing a person. Don't you think that with this, you really could get more insight on who a person is? Yes is the answer; and it will always remain yes, at least for a very long time. For this reason, you should be very careful on what addiction this partner has, this is very important. There are ones, like substances that will not only make this person a wrong person, but will also endanger your life if you tend to be with this person. Some of his addictions too will let you have a better understanding of him to be able to make a decision on being in a relationship with him or not.

His addiction will make you to get to know the kind of person you are in a relationship with. Assuming this person is addicted to liquor, or drugs; and you think that his addiction does not really matter on the kind of person he is? It matters and it goes further to tell his disposition. You may see it as something that really can be cured by visiting a rehab and all that if it gets serious. Or that your conclusion might be that such addiction is fun to him. If he is addicted to something that is bad, you really should start seeing this person as a wrong person, unless he makes a turn from the addiction. Some people who are addicts although taken to rehab show tendency that they might return back to that addiction especially when trouble hits them. And people that have great addiction on something else always show a high dependency rate. They are only satisfied or happy when they fulfill that attachment they have with such a substance. I was reading one of the national dailies the other time; I came across the news of a onetime popular musician, who now roams the street. From his wife's confession, that addiction did not start newly; he was an addict even before they got married. She narrated how wonderful a man he was, even though he has frustrated her for so long with his addiction; and now she would no longer cope. She moved on, and divorced him. Too bad that she has been in a hurting relationship for long trying to endure while she patiently waited for a change that never came. This will tell you that some of these addictions are somehow humanly not possible to stop if one engages in them. A mature person who is qualified enough to make a better partner should

YES, ONLY TO THE RIGHT PERSON

not show a sign of having to depend strictly on something particularly to be able to live a happy life.

If this person lives on substance that he finds it hard to do without, then you really need to give it a rethink. It is a warning sign that this person will likely turn into something you never can imagine. And most people that are chronic addicts always go back to the substances when they face challenges. They don't really want to face challenge squarely like a mature person, always looking for something to assuage their pains and solve the problems for them. Is this the kind of person you will like to be in a relationship with, someone that will be such a coward to solve problems and withstand pressures? Chronic addiction should not be seen as lifestyle; it should be seen as a disease, too hard to cure. It tends to expose how mentally and emotionally weak a person is. Ask yourself, if one cannot get over sadness unless he takes a substance, how will such a person solve a serious problem in a relationship when it occurs? This person loses his job and tries few times to get another but it didn't work out. Instead of sitting down to rejig his plans and come out with another formula to solving that problem once and for all, he goes back to the drinking parlor to drink himself to stupor. Does it not show how weak and stupid he is to make a good partner?

You really need a partner that is emotionally and mentally strong enough to face a challenge like a man. You need one who is strong enough to rise above challenges and not shy away from them. You need one that will always be at his senses all the time to do things rightly. And do not forget that someone who sits down and thinks when there is trouble, instead of sitting down to drink, has that quality that a right partner should have. This will make you to look into the addiction of your partner and see what kind of addiction it is and how strongly attached he is to such addiction. This will tell you how serious his situation is. Imagine when you have a partner and he goes on to tell you that he is always happy when he takes a particular substance. Don't you think that if he didn't take such substance that he will be sad? And being sad, will likely put pressures on the relationship as well. What if when issue arise, instead of opening up and finding solution, this person goes behind to depend on a particular substance to make him forget that worry. Will that not make you see the reason that he needs that substance more than he needs you to sooth his pains? This reminds me when we were kids, our addictions were chocolate and biscuits, these we didn't joke with, and our happiness depended on them. It got so badly then that even if you were a threat to our life, get us these stuffs and we would feel relaxed around you, easily falling prey. Beat us black and blue and get us those stuffs, the matter is solved, we won't care what harm you have done to us. This only exposed our weakness as kids. The same with adults, addiction exposes their own weakness, making them kids mentally to be in a relationship with.

As a matter of fact, one whose happiness, wellbeing; and life revolve around a particular substance, always makes a bad partner. A rational being does not hold on to just a mere substance for existence because that might really be scarce tomorrow plunging such one into a mess. And for that, he avoids being so attached to something else solely. Earlier said, there are some substances when addicted to them, not only endanger the person, but also endanger the people around him. And those who depend on this harmful substance to be happy and can't do without it, always pose a threat to people that are close to them when agitated. This person's memory is always altered when he takes such substance and you think that one day it won't go out of hand? It will. A day will come when an increased challenge will set in, and this person will as well increase the quantity, to sooth his pain; this might go out of hand. With this too, you could as well know what to expect from this person. If a person's life will be so endangered by the kind of addiction he engages in, then how unwise it will be to live with a person that will soon meet his doom. Don't just take it as his lifestyle that it has nothing to do with who he really is, it has a great deal to not only tell who he is, but also influences who he is and will turn out to be.

YES, ONLY TO THE RIGHT PERSON

Sadly, some may be addicted to sex and that shapes their life, they tend to not get enough of it. The more this person gets the little quantity than he needs, the more he will likely try to get it anywhere else. Taking a deep thought about what one is addicted to and how strong the addiction is, will give you more insight about this person you are in a relationship with to see if making serious commitment will be wise. There are other of this person's addictions that you have to think whether they will either be of benefit to you and the relationship, or harmful. If you find them harmful, then such a person could also be harmful to you in a relationship.

Tool 11

The Person's Grooming

Don't bother telling me, your appearance has said it all. And if you go on to put up a defense telling me you dress just like others. You again implicate yourself telling me that you are mentally a kid to be an adult."
- O.D. Chimex

The care taken in personal appearance summarizes the word grooming. This goes a step further to let you know what really a kind of person he is or will be, although some people don't take into consideration this fact. Dressing and appearance talk more of a person than words and actions will. When I was much younger, I judged people only based on their words and actions; but as I mature it occurred to me that I could not even wait for a person to speak or act before I could decipher what likely a kind of person he might be. As soon as I got this fact, I became very attentive to people's appearance anywhere I am. This helped me a lot to avoid whole lots of troubles; although misconception might as well occur, that will be very minimal. This grooming goes with not just what one wears, but how one puts the clothes and other things combined that make up someone's total appearance. It goes from head to toe appearance of a person. This is very important; that is why some professions try as much as possible to introduce dress code related to their work. They know quite well that this will give the public an inkling understanding of what the profession is all about and what respect to accord it.

Even at this, not everybody in a particular profession will have the same grooming even though they might be putting on the same dress code. This is simply because of the divergence in personalities. And this divergence shows not only the mental status, it also shows the understanding and character of a person toward that particular profession, and as well, real life. And this grooming goes on to accentuate their daily life, and not just work. I once worked in a tertiary institution, hospital precisely, where you see lots of professionals ranging from doctors, to pharmacist, medical laboratory scientists, and radiographer, and so on and so forth. Within the institution also were other groups, ranging from administrative staff, skilled and unskilled labourers, and medical students as well. Those in professional group, including the medical students were expected to dress corporately at all times, always putting on their ties, for men. But not all that put on such corporate attire looked corporately, simply because of the way each individual grooms. Some dressed smartly, and some really, were smarter. Some also looked stupid because of the stupid ways they groomed, inclusive of their hairstyles. But in the end, I found out that that divergence in grooming says a lot about different personalities and mentalities.

In this serious quest to finding a right partner, a person's grooming should be used as a tool in understanding a whole lot more about a person. It will let you into this person's mental status, his overall understanding of life, and his characters and dispositions. You really need to take this very seriously if you want to have a thorough and holistic knowledge about a person. Though some aspect of grooming might be affected by external factors, but then, there will always be a link between a person and his grooming, this is inextricable. Get some bankers the best of suits and ties; you will see some putting their ties and trousers precariously. Even the way some make their clothes will tell you more about them. This shows more of a person without gentility, this tells you about this person than you need to be told. A person's hairstyle, the makeup, and the jewelries will further show you a whole lot about the person with regards to materialism and what becomes important in his life. Someone might portray himself to be a very humble one, but his grooming might reveal to you that humility is lacking. A person may always assume reasonableness; then only his grooming will confirm that. People go a long way to show you how erratic they are in life by their grooming as well, becoming a chameleon in styles. This will make you to be very alert as to those perfidious actions that go in contrary to the person's grooming. Who and what one is, should always be reflected in the way the person grooms. Although ignorance and illiteracy might have an influence in one's grooming, but then it as well tells you that this person is either of this. And where there is no external factor, it shows that internal factors have overbearing influence on the person. Have you wondered why a particular set of miscreants always groom in a particular manner? This is simply because they have the same disposition and that is why they tend to groom in the same manner; they are the same inwardly.

You have no excuses to give when dating a wrong person if you give no attention to the person's grooming. It talks so much about the person's qualities unseen. Take for instance with regards to a person's mental status, it shows in his grooming. Take a look at a mentally deranged person; don't you see a striking resemblance with his grooming and his mental state? People, who are very smart and intelligent intrinsically, will always show that in the way they groom. And as well, people who are not too smart, dull and all that, will on the other hand, show you that as well in their grooming. For this reason, employer's first assessment of the employee is his appearance. Dress stupidly and have the best grades, you might lose that job interview, just on the first call into the interview room, you will be walked out.

YES, ONLY TO THE RIGHT PERSON

Financial capacity has only but insignificant contribution on grooming; mental capacity has more contribution. If you have seen a religious extremist or a suicide bomber few minutes prior to carrying out a dastardly attack, his grooming will tell you that this person has lost a whole lot mentally. So while you watch this person's behaviours as well, pay also attention to his grooming, it might reveal to you more things about this person than what you might be told.

I had whole lots of friends who keep telling me that they don't care about grooming, that they will actually influence their partner in this regard. And I asked then, if you improve on a person's grooming, will you as well improve the person's mental capacity? Give different individuals the same wears, shoes, and makeup; then ask then to put them on. You will come to understand how intelligent they are, in having a good combination of those things. And people, who tend to be arrogant and have atom of gangsterism in them, always show that in their grooming as well.

Another thing the grooming will tell you about this person is his understanding of life in general. What matters in his life and what matters not, grooming will tell you that. Some will tell you by their grooming that they can go hungry just to put on a particular clothe; and you think this person will make a good partner? If one could not understand what things are more important in life, then how could he understand the importance of a relationship? Understanding of life goes a long way to tell you more about the person's attitude toward the trends not just in his environment, but also his location and the world in general. If one understands this, the reasonableness in his grooming will attest to that. This will give you a clue on how this person tends to handle things in life. Does he handle things with reasonableness or is he such a person that is either too rigid, or too flexible? His grooming will tell you that as well.

So forget about what he puts up to deceive you, his grooming will tell you the truth more. Some who are very rigid in life does not really understand the dynamism in the world, so as to adjust when it is necessary. And you think this anachronistic person will understand the dynamism in a relationship and adjust when it is needed? A person by his grooming also show how flexible he could be, unreasonably changing just as a chameleon when such change is not that necessary. Don't you think that you will continue to find this person too complex to understand? New week, new character and new personality. More reason you have to take the person's grooming very seriously to be able to understand those characters that might likely be visible only when you have crossed the boundary in a relationship. And that boundary is serious commitment, likely marriage.

Another area which this grooming tends to throw more light is on the person's behavior. Your appearance tells people more than what you have to tell them. And if you go on to defend your grooming telling me that you dress just to be like others; then it shows you are mentally a kid to be an adult. What a person wears, hairstyles, and all that, tell you a whole lot about a person's lifestyle. I had this course mate who was a flirt, and he always went about, grooming in a way that showed he wanted attention all the time. He was so obsessed with his appearance then, that he could spend even his school fees on his appearance, just to look good. Do you still need a soothsayer to tell you that this person will soon show you he is the wrong person? He goes on spending money on you; and you have concluded already that he is so generous. Wait until you appraise his appearance, it will tell you the truth. Look at his grooming; he spends lots of money to make you look good, and he looks so poorly. He is only a conman that wants to impress you or entice you with wealth; this person is really dead stingy.

He spends most of his fortune on his appearance making you believe he has got the money, whereas this man is broke. It is simple, he is a smart liar and fake too. And he spends just on himself not

YES, ONLY TO THE RIGHT PERSON

minding if you look like a tramp, then you need to watch out for this selfish person as a partner. Don't let few things make you to come to conclusion that you have known this person well enough to make a commitment like marriage, things like grooming will go a long way to tell you more about what sort of person he is. And if you as well beam your searchlight to his grooming, you will no doubt come to connect his grooming to all other behaviors he has. The ones still not let out; you will see them clearly with your mind eyes. Don't wait till he tells you, let his appearance tell you first; and when he finally tells you, if they are not in discrepancy.

Part Four
Making Yourself That Right Person

Introduction

"Everything that irritates us about others can lead us to an understanding of ourselves." - **Carl Jung.**

How wise to know that when one is pointing an accusing finger on another person, the rest of the fingers point back at the person. When I was making research prior to writing this book, I came across several write-ups that suggested that the best way to know the right person is one working to be that right person; this form the basis for this part. In all the parts of this book we have discussed the other person, now this part we will discuss about you and that is you reading this book. Balance should always be maintained in life and that balance is talking not just the other person but also talking about yourself. For the fact that you have seen what you need to be mindful of in a relationship; then the onus lies on you to also be mindful of yourself as well, for the other person to also find you worthy. And everything that irritates you about others can lead you to an understanding of yourself. In this part, you will read various ways to work on yourself so as to get you better and improved to make the right one also for another person. And just like a Confucius quote: "When you see a good person, think of becoming like her/him. When you see someone not so good, reflect on your own weak points."

Step 1

Your Mindset

"We are addicted to our thoughts. We cannot change anything if we cannot change our thinking."
- Santosh Kalwar.

Things that you do most times come from your mind; though you might be influenced by your disposition. In the advent of globalization, people have taken the habit of just picking most of the things happening around them feeding them into their mind and then turning them into an idiosyncrasy and eventually a way of life. Some do this unknowingly, others do it wittingly. Whichever way is the case, the truth remains that what you feed your mind constantly with will definitely affect your speech and in the long run influencing your behavior becoming your disposition. And how do you expect to be a right person in a relationship when you have a wrong mindset? This is the reason behind someone regretting an action of his, if being brought to his notice. He knows quite well that that is not the real person he is inside, but the overwhelming influence surrounding him has made him to be what he really was not born with. You have read a lot about qualities of a right person to be in a relationship with, and those danger signs, moving down to better ways to knowing the real attitude of someone. This is the time you should also have in mind that you ought

YES, ONLY TO THE RIGHT PERSON

to make yourself that right person so as to be acceptable, just like other person will be acceptable by you, if the person meets the basic criteria. Your mindset could be your habitual way of thinking, the belief that affects your way of thinking influencing your behaviour and ultimately impacting on the type of partner you will make in a relationship. No matter how good a person might be for you in a relationship, you must also be good so as to be accepted by the person as the right person for him too.

I always believe that we all are rational beings in the sense that we differ from other animals in thinking and in behaviours too. This should always be brought to bear in all your way of doing things and in relationship. For this reason, knowledge is spew out for us to avail ourselves of them and be better refined and ultimately be better humans and better partners. This knowledge and information come from family, circular source, religion, culture, and from the world through improved internet and the media. But despite all these avalanche of information and knowledge, you sometimes wonder why some behave the way they do. Sometimes instead of the said knowledge to impact positively on the person, you see the person going the other way. What is the cause of this discrepancy, you might wonder? Some will be perplexed that despite this person's level of education, he still exhibits such nasty character. The problem lies with how and what knowledge and information are given, that affect their mindset negatively. You begin to see that despite those information and knowledge, this person is yet to have a better character. This is because the person has a total different mindset as a result of negative things stuffed in it. It might also be as a result of the conflict between his disposition and what information he gets. Knowledge and information are made to have in impact in a person either negatively or positively. For this reason, one should be mindful of whatever mindset he is building as a result of this knowledge and information, to avoid contradicting his real selves. Having at the back of your mind that you are a rational being will make you to taste whatever knowledge and information that you pick knowingly and unknowingly then applying them rightly. These knowledge and information will affect your mindset making you act in way that tends to portray you a bad person or a good person; contradicting yourself with your character. You may have an awful disposition, but you can as well be refined to be better than you are if you allow these knowledge and information to affect your mindset positively.

If your mindset is so affected negatively and becomes in opposite direction with what is generally acceptable, then what magic do you expect to happen, other than acting and speaking what you think? This distorted mindset; you go a long way to bring into any relationship, thereby making yourself a wrong person even though by nature you might be a right person. This is the reason you should know that this transformation starts with reforming your mindset so as to begin than process of being a right person. Those things you read about the good and bad signs in a relationship, have you sat down to think of areas you need adjustment in your mindset so as to reflect them in your life? If there is any, the adjustment should start with your mindset this moment. This reformation should start within your mindset if you are truthful to yourself. If your mindset is transformed, it will be very easy for the effect to trickle down to your speech and your characters. The issue lies on how to make this mindset transformed if you think that there is need for that. It is very simple to build a powerful positive mindset with those information and knowledge that are coming into you. This reformation will not only reflect on your speeches and characters, but will also remind you of that bad character whenever it comes out of you. With this mindset, you will continue to make adjustments, and be at alert to develop those wonderful qualities that will make you a right person in a relationship.

For you to be at alert as to what influences your mindset, you need to get your mind off things that are not really wholesome, be it

YES, ONLY TO THE RIGHT PERSON

information, knowledge or entertainment. Things that by nature are against humanity and that the greater number in the society abhors, even if some few people might be practicing it. If those things hurt others, you really need to stop letting such things form your mindset so that it may not form a mental picture that you will always act upon. You might not know the impact this might be having on your mindset until it forms your behaviour if care is not taken. For sometimes now, I tend to read lots about people that were once good, but suddenly they turned to monster or extremist due to the information loaded in them which affected them negatively. And this information and knowledge influenced their mindset so badly that they became a threat to other humans. They themselves practicing it know that it is wrong, but their mindset has written a script for them to act. The fact is that, these people would have not gone that badly if they have been given the right knowledge and information. Even if they have such disposition, they would have been curtailed and checkmated if they had taken the right thing that will form their mindset. The entertainment you watch might really be making you a wrong person to be in a relationship with, likewise your choice of friends. Things like these might be telling you that you need a particular bad character to succeed. But if you will hate such in a partner, will it not be wise to hate practicing such too? The more the bad influence, the more your mindset changes to worse, and in turn, you will become a wrong person to be in a relationship with even when you have found a right person. How will you expect that right person to be in a relationship with you when you are the wrong person for him? This right person will find out one day, and will brand you wrong person leaving you behind with broken feelings.

Keeping a balance is always the best in taking positive information, knowledge and other thins that shape your mindset. The rationality in you will make you to taste out whatever information or knowledge to see what benefit it will have on a greater number of people, you inclusive, and also people that are closer to you. Whatever knowledge and information that have greater harm than good, and hurt others, should be questioned to come into your mindset, even if they make you feel benefited. Don't be deceived by others to load your mindset with things that you know are wrong. Some may have a bad experience and will try to allow that experience to have negative influence on them thereby taking a bad mindset as a defense against reoccurrence. They tend to forget that not everybody will treat them just like a particular bad person has treated them. If that be the case, why taking to a mindset to hurt innocent ones simply because someone or few people have acted badly towards you? Remember this mindset is like your engine and when it gets bad, it begins to affect the whole car. And when your mindset is so filled with things that are harmful, you end up not making progress. How will a car with very fanciful body run very well when the engine is so filled with dirty diesel or oil? For it to get running and be reliable, that dirty engine should be washed thoroughly off that dirt. You should wash your mindset and be ready not to allow things unwholesome to occupy your mindset. When you do that, you are home and dry to likely allow positive knowledge and information influence good behaviour in you which will make you a right person to be in a relationship with. If you have read lots of good qualities about a right partner, why not begin to make such qualities form your mindset so as to speak it and act it. And those bad qualities let it also be taken off your mindset if you have any in you.

Don't just sit down to monitor other person if he will be good to make a better partner or not. Monitor yourself too so as to make a better partner to other person as well. And the first place to keep on guard for is your mindset, which will likely influence your speech and your character. Even if, intrinsically you think that you might be good, don't underestimate the power of your mindset influencing you to be bad when bad information and wrong knowledge is pushed into you. Your age matters not in this regard, you could be a monster the next minute that is because of the complexity in human nature. It is obvious

YES, ONLY TO THE RIGHT PERSON

that when you allow good things to form your mindset, you have every tendency to act those good things. They become you and you become them, in the long run your behavior will continue to let it out. About the bad things that you allow to form part of your mindset, they can really be crowded out by more good things. Take it as a responsibility to work on what you think and believe habitually, that are bad, so as not to be a bad person looking for a good person. Be that good person looking for another good person; and let like-pole attract like-pole. If your mindset is worked up, the job is not totally done; the next should be your speech which will be discussed in the next topic.

Step 2

Your Speech

"We speak not only to tell other people what we think, but to tell ourselves what we think. Speech is a part of thought." - **Oliver Sacks.**

Like that quotation above, your mindset will become your speech sooner or later. What you speak all the time might be what you act sometimes, because it is your thought. It is always like that; what a person thinks all the time is always what he may speak sometimes; and that is the way it will trickle down to the way the person behaves. You words and the way you say them, tend to not just become how you will act, it goes a long way to tell others who you are. What you say and how you say it also contribute to your personality and relationship with others. People could get healed or hurt by your words. And this makes it very important for one to also work on his speech so as to have that perfect reformation needed in order to be that right person. If one wants to make that thorough change, then his speech should be paid attention to. No matter how wonderful you are, your speech could render you bad, scaring people away from you. No one will like to be with someone that says different thing from what his personality is. There should be harmony between your thought and your speech trickling down to your actions. You may be tricked to think

YES, ONLY TO THE RIGHT PERSON

that it is not necessary to watch your speech, but it is very important in life. With your words alone, people will categorize you. The same way it is in a relationship, you might really love someone so much and have shown the qualities of a right person to be in a relationship with, but your words might just make you a wrong person. If one continues to be hurt by your words, then you are as well saying in essence that you are not the right one. And if your choice of words contradicts you always, then you will lose at the end. It is the reason the policemen on coming to arrest a suspect, keep warning him to be silent or be judged by whatever he might say. Though imperfection might always make it almost impossible for you to avoid saying what you really don't mean sometimes, caution should be taken. Being careful enough will save you a whole lot, not just you but others who might suffer as a result of such mistake. This makes it imperative; having worked on your mindset, the next point of call is your choice of words and the tone with which such words are said. Paying attention to these is a way to show that you want to put up the fight in trying to be a right person for a relationship.

Watching your words goes a long way to save you from being pushed unknowingly to act just like you speak. One who is fond of saying always that he will slap someone, will one day slap the person. Your words could drive you to action; that is the power of words. For this reason you really need to be on the guard to always keep an eye on your speech so as to be that right person for a relationship. It is always good to make your words so soft and sweet so that you could as well take them back if need be. Do not just talk because you know how to talk and do not just talk just because you have something to talk. Even when provoked to talk, you should first of all talk with your brain before talking with your mouth. An adage says: "Before you talk, you should firstly taste those words." Taste them if they will affect you or the other person negatively. By tasting them, you will assume the one receiving those words firstly. If you will be stung by such words you are about telling someone else, reasonableness demands that you should not say such, if you want to make a good person in a relationship. And this shows that you are really working on becoming someone that a partner will like to be with. Developing consciousness when talking is possible, and when you do, you will find out that your words are spoken out of deep thought.

Another area to work on is your tone of voice when saying such words. If you shout 'sorry,' to someone, then it makes no difference. Working on your speech demands that you should as well work on the tone with which you say a word. It is never justifiable to always say that you have a loud voice therefore you shout words. In no way will you shout when talking to yourself, yet you keep saying you have loud voice, only when talking to others. Even a nasty word when said with a very low tone could not be weighty as when said in a shouting manner. Words said forcefully in a very high tone could even trigger anger in you then pushing you to action. And being carefully selective on the words you speak is always good; applying caution when making facial expression and gestures when speaking is good as well. For these to be possible you should pay attention to other external factors influencing your speech, your tone, your facial expressions and gestures. Some of these external factors are what you listen to, what you watch, what you read, and what you think. The same way they will affect your mindset is the same way they will affect your speech, either negatively or positively.

You might have seen or heard people that believe that what they listen to will not influence them; they are telling themselves lie. Ears take whatever you listen to, to the brain to analyze it based on the already stored knowledge. The knowledge you have acquired through those specified avenues discussed in the chapter above. And as specified in that chapter, when you must have balanced what you take in to make your mindset, you will be in a better position to avoid negative things that will always affect your speech. These negative things you listen to and think might not really mean anything to you, but they will continue

YES, ONLY TO THE RIGHT PERSON

to be what you will always speak most of the times. And the more you get to stuff your ear with such crass the more the brain absorbs them making them to be your speech most of the time. This has every tendency to become what you act knowingly or unknowingly. This makes it very serious to begin to sieve through what you listen to so that it will not affect your speech negatively making you a wrong person.

What you watch all the time also form part of what you will continue to speak all the time. I knew these kids in the neighborhood; they always liked to discuss wrestling simply because they watched it constantly. Adults are not left out in this regard; they tend to always talk about what they watch. Imagine during a world cup season what forms major part of discussion of adult football lovers. No other thing than the matches being played, the ones that will be played; so does it happen to all of us. What you watch all the time forms major part of what you will be speaking all the time; and for this reason, caution should be taken. Working on the things that you watch being selective to pick out positive ones will likely make one to speak graciously in order to make a wonderful person. You want a right person that will always be what he says, consoling you with his words and not tearing you. The same way you have to work on your speech so as to be in harmony with what you really claim to be, to also influence what you act; building your partner and not tearing the person down with words.

What you read is also very important in this regard. They still go into the same place which is the brain, molding your mindset which will in turn become your speech. We get knowledge mostly by reading; and this knowledge could be like a bad food taken. It goes into your system and causes a rumbling in your stomach; and before you know it, you start to vomit. What you vomit will be just exactly the food taken; likewise reading unwholesome things, vomiting unwholesome words. Read good things which will not make you to vomit, rather will get digested, nourish your body and make you always be in a pleasant mood to talk pleasant things. Have in mind that you will also want a right partner to talk pleasantly and act pleasantly; so should you, for you both to make right persons for each other and make a good relationship. So working on your speech is very important so as not to start acting those negative things that you say.

And your thinking is not exempted, you should be mindful of what you think. Sometimes you find out that the mind can also be independent being affected by what we could not lay hands on, maybe feelings at the moment may contribute. This unconscious attitude done by the brain should always not be allowed to linger if they are moving toward negativity. The more you think such negative things, you begin making them up in words as output. Giving thought to positive things always help to cushion this effect caused as a result of feelings or other things impulsive. It is unheard of to imagine of talking what you have not thought of, be at alert to avert this chain reaction. Your thought will always engender your speech. And this negative speech will in turn affect you and the other person adding to what you will always act. You might not always think of positive things; but then, always force yourself not to think of negative things.

In the fight not to act negatively, words should be put on check so as to be that organized person, reasonable enough to bring in harmony his words and action, to bear in his good personality. Even when others around you or the environment is making you to speak in a particular way, the rationality in you should make you to apply caution. If possible; avoiding coming in contact with such triggers, is always the best thing to do. As said earlier, once in a while you may succumb to imperfection, but when such happens, don't make it a way of life to continue speaking negatively. The effort to change and be a better a person should be sincere, especially when you speak and someone gets hurt, contrite attitude and reparation are needed. This earnest effort to make a change in yourself, when started with working on your mindset, your speech, then coming down to your character, is always the best approach. Your work plan should start with looking intently into those

YES, ONLY TO THE RIGHT PERSON

wonderful qualities a right person should exhibit, then attuning your speech in line with them. The next is to look at those danger signs, then detaching your speech from them. And finally your character should reflect the change, harmonizing it with all the changes you have made. In the next topic, we will discuss further how this should be possible, with regards to your character.

Step 3

Your Character

"We are builders of our own characters. We have different positions, spheres, capacities, privileges, different work to do in the world; different temporal fabrics to raise; but we are all alike in this...all are architects of fate." - **John Fothergill Waterhouse Ware.**

"Let me be; this is the way I behave, I was born that way." This some people give as an excuse when being told of a particular character they exhibit. Such a person I term to be unintelligible, because he forgets that characters are developed and could as well be picked directly or indirectly. If one maintains his ground that it is his disposition to behave in a particular manner, such a person thinks he can't change; then he better move into the bush and live with the rest of his colleagues. Though we have disposition, but it has always been noticed that the way most people behave is as a result of what they make of their life. Even if one has a bad disposition that will not form the basis to find it hard to improve on his character. Improvement on the character could even make that bad disposition toothless to be having overwhelming influence on someone. When one is serious to work on his character, he might find out that those things he thought were inherent are not, they may just be characters

YES, ONLY TO THE RIGHT PERSON

developed. For this reason, it is very necessary to work on your character to either regain your real self or be a refined you. When you are eager to find the right person to be in a relationship with, you should also be eager to make yourself a right person. If everybody keeps being the wrong person, tell me how one will get to find a right person to be in a relationship with. This will form the basis to watch what your characters are and see if they need to be worked on; this watching, those first two sections of this book have made it easy to do. Assuming you found out that the aggressiveness you have, makes you a bad partner; will that not push you to work on yourself? That, every wise person will do, and not wanting others to be gentle, while he goes on being aggressive. Will it not amount to foolishness when one knows a bad flaw he has and keeps telling people to be mindful of such his bad attitude? It is like a person with a very bad disease telling people that he has such disease. The other day, I was talking to a person and he told me in black and white; "I am hot-tempered don't provoke me." And I replied him; "You are stupid, don't provoke yourself."

Reasonableness demands that one should keep working on his awful character when being brought to his notice, instead of announcing them for people to avoid him in that regard. Don't just read this text to see another person, use it also as a mirror to see yourself, and areas you need serious adjustment. Those things that when someone displays will make you to distance yourself from the person, distance yourself from those characters as well. Try your possible best to take them out of you so that others will not distance themselves from you. As a boy, I sometimes found it hard to understand why my parents punished me. To me, they were just strict and wanted me to be sad sometimes. They had no justification for punishing me that was my thinking. But then, I was not aware of some of my bad characters they wanted to correct. As I grew up, it occurred to me that I really have characters that I should constantly work on to drop and also ones to improve upon so that I will achieve a real me, refined too. This reformation is very necessary because those things hurt others; so for me to be at peace with others, I must take those characters away entirely replacing them with wonderful ones. If I don't, I would just be an island, separated from others. People who have this mindset not to be isolated from others are always at relative peace with others. They try to take away those characters they have that will irritate others; this should be your own resolve this minute. Don't just fold your hands to read about qualities of a right person and the danger signs that make one a wrong person. Uproot from yourself those danger signs if you have them, and develop in you those positive qualities, the ones you don't have. You can never be certain that you are the way you are, until you try to look at things from the other angle. You might be very surprised the new person you will become, and that may be that real you that has been suppressed by just situations and external influences. For instance, if one could be so generous to himself, always giving himself the best and anything he wants, why won't such one be generous toward other person? If one could not beat himself when angry, then why should such one beat another person when expressing his anger? This will tell you that someone of things one might think is inherent might really not be. Thank God, that by nature humans are camera, they could just snap a particular object and make it a picture. When you start building a wonderful character, it could change you turning you to a wonderful person which you will always bring out as an output.

Everything that irritates you about another person, will go a long way telling you what will also irritate others about you. Having this in mind will push you to try your possible best to work on, either improving on your good qualities, or taking away from you bad qualities. If you are really telling yourself the truth, watching someone to see how good he will make a good partner is not just enough. You are involved too to watch yourself on how good you will make a good partner, and it is another person that will tell you. When you exhibit bad characters, others will either be telling it directly or indirectly to

YES, ONLY TO THE RIGHT PERSON

you; and as a rational being it behoves on you to change. If a mature person comes up now to claim that he knows not his characters, then the person is deceiving himself. Whatever bad, one is doing to another person he knows it; he will feel and see that other person hurting. Whatever good you think and wish yourself, you are also required to think and wish it to others by your characters toward them. Reading this book should be like a football team where there are two groups, the trainer and the trainee, having a kind of symbiotic relationship. The trainers in as much as they train the trainees, getting to know and select the best to make up a team; they are also keeping fit during the course of the training so as to make them better trainers. In fact some trainers do learn a lot from their trainees in the course of watching out who will make a better player; they as well improve themselves. Read to know the right person as well as read to learn how to be a right person. And this should also be brought to bear in a relationship, studying a person to see if he would make a better person, you improve yourself by learning those qualities that will make you a better person. In that process, you keep dropping those characters in you that you know will make you a bad partner to that other person.

Imagine you are a parent, and you expect your kids to always be kind and generous, while you are mean and stingy. How on earth do you think that it will work? A snake will always give birth to a snake and not a sheep, a bad teacher will never raise good student. For that reason that you are also in a relationship to make this person a better person, will only be possible when you have good to give to this other person. Those gifts of positive influence will be seen as serious and taken only when you have those gifts as yours. There is no way someone who has no car will give a gift of car to another person, he will be seen as either a thief or a borrower. You will never give what you don't have. If you are stingy, you can never influence someone to be generous. Likewise if you are lazy, and you think you will make this partner to work hard? Only a person suffering from delusion will think that way. So watching your characters so as to improve on them is very important in making yourself the right person to be in a relationship with. Don't just beam your searchlight on the other person's character; beam it on your own as well to position yourself for being the right person. This will also be alluded to a particular rule in the bible called the golden rule, and it states: "Whatever you want men to do to you, do to them as well." And whatever you want men to stop doing, stop doing it yourself.

And this reminds me of what a father used to do to teach his kids about life virtues. Whenever he wants to teach them about generosity, he will first get a gift and share them among his family members, irrespective of how little it was. Then later, he will organize them, citing the action he performed few hours ago. That was not just an organized act; the family watched him continue to prove to be generous to them in providing for their needs. With this method, his kids came to feel it and not just listen to it as just a sermon. When an iron is continuously heated and beaten, that iron no matter how hard it is will start to have another shape according to the beating. If you continue working on your character, no doubt, you will have another shape as you want. And in the long run you will develop qualities that are endearing and wonderful to attract another. In fact being the right person demands that you should be fair; and that fairness warrants that you work on your character as well so as to make a right person for the other person. So whatever irritates you about another person, will give you an insight about yourself so as not to go on irritating others. The effort to make yourself the right person will never go in vain if you are serious about it, and that will pave more chance for you to have a wonderful relationship when you have seen the right person. And just as the heading portrays, knowing the right person will never be complete unless you make yourself that right person too.

YES, ONLY TO THE RIGHT PERSON

www.ingramcontent.com/pod-product-compliance
Lightning Source LLC
Chambersburg PA
CBHW070053080526
44586CB00013B/1042